CROWOOD METALWORKING GUIDES

# THE MINI-LATHE

CROWOOD METALWORKING GUIDES

# THE MINI-LATHE

## NEIL M. WYATT

THE CROWOOD PRESS

First published in 2016 by
The Crowood Press Ltd
Ramsbury, Marlborough
Wiltshire SN8 2HR

enquiries@crowood.com

**www.crowood.com**

This impression 2022

© The Crowood Press 2016

**British Library Cataloguing-in-Publication Data**
A catalogue record for this book is available from the British Library.

ISBN 978 1 78500 128 4

Typeset by Servis Filmsetting Ltd, Stockport, Cheshire
Printed and bound in India by Parksons Graphics Pvt. Ltd.

# Contents

# 1    Why a Mini-Lathe?

Ask a dozen model engineers 'what is the best lathe for me?' and you will get two dozen answers! One of the finest writers on the hobby, Edgar Westbury (E.T.W.), said: 'The so-called "ideal lathe" is in practice a romantic myth.' He had the perception to realize we all have different needs and the best lathe for each of us will always be a compromise. Mini-lathes provide capacity, capability and many useful features at an affordable price. They may not be 'ideal' for everyone but they have proven the best route into hobby engineering for tens or hundreds of thousands.

Most modern books on small lathes have been written by authors more familiar with larger machines or 'classic' older lathes. Inevitably, their experience with larger machines colours their approach to these machines.

My own lathe, in regular use for the past sixteen years, is a Clarke CL300M mini-lathe (Fig. 1.1). This is one of the main machines featured in this book. In using the machine I have been pleasantly surprised – while some aspects of the lathe are made to keep costs down, it is rigid, accurate and reliable.

This book deals with what I have discovered during those sixteen years of use, from choosing a lathe, basic safety and setting it up properly, through a range of basic turning skills, to tackling some more challenging machining operations and making useful accessories. I can't guarantee every single point I cover will apply to every variant of mini-lathe but, by the same token, many of the general principles will apply to any lathe of similar size.

I have made numerous modifications and additions to my machine; some of these are 'standard' upgrades, others are of my own devising. Be assured that none of them are essential to using a mini-lathe but also recognize the basic machine has plenty of scope for modification and tuning if you are, like me, a 'tweaker'.

This book gives most dimensions in metric and imperial units. These are not intended to be exact equivalents, especially where a dimension is given as a guide. For example, a thousandth of an inch is exactly 0.0254mm but I may well write something such as 'about 0.02mm (0.001in)'.

I would like to thank the many fellow mini-lathe users who both knowingly and unwittingly have helped me over the years with advice, ideas and guidance. In particular, the writings and ideas of Alastair Sinclair and Mike Cox have been a source of ideas and inspiration. They say there are no new ideas in engineering and I apologize if I have unintentionally copied anyone without giving due credit.

I would like to thank Arc Euro Trade, Axminster Tools & Machinery, Chester Machine Tools, Eccentric Engineering, Machine Mart and Warco for permission to use photographs of their machines, as well as SIEG for permission to use extracts from its user manual.

Finally, for a book like this I also needed access to an unmodified machine and various accessories to demonstrate certain points. I would like to thank Ketan Swali of Arc Euro Trade for the opportunity to use its studio to photograph a new, unmodified SIEG mini-lathe and also for his advice on the various subtleties and technical aspects of these worthy machines.

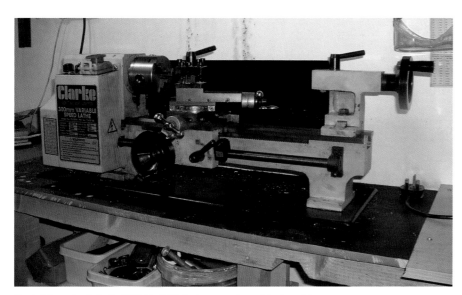

*Fig. 1.1 The author's Clarke CL300M mini-lathe in more or less original condition.*

# 2  Safety

Some readers will groan at this point but, unless one has seen the aftermath of an industrial accident, is easy to be blasé about the risks associated with machine tools.

Lathes are one of the slower and quieter tools so it is easy to get complacent about the risks they pose. However, complacency is a cause of accidents. Even a mini-lathe is capable of causing serious injury from sharp tools, flying swarf (debris) and collisions or entanglement with moving parts. Don't panic, though. Lathe safety mostly means using your common sense and keeping the working area clean and tidy. Here are some pointers towards the safe use of any workshop lathe but, remember, safety is your responsibility and if you are not sure – ask!

## Emergency Stop

Make sure you are familiar with the emergency stop button. It does no harm to use this to stop the lathe in day-to-day operations and the more familiar you are with using it, the faster you will be able to hit it in an emergency (Fig. 2.1).

## Protective Equipment

Unlike many machine tools, lathes do not demand a lot in the way of personal protective equipment. The HSE recommends eye protection is worn when using a lathe and if cutting something such as brass, which can send a vertical shower of small chips into the air, full eye protection is essential (Fig. 2.2). For most turning, many people find a pair of safety spectacles are sufficient but bear in mind that flying swarf is not the only risk – it is possible for loose work pieces to fly out of the chuck at high speed.

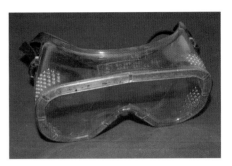

*Fig. 2.2 A pair of safety googles is an excellent investment.*

## Electricity

As with any electrical equipment, take the usual care with leads and around the electrical parts of the machine, bearing in mind lathes move and wires can be drawn into machinery. Ensure the plug is wired correctly and any fuses that blow are replaced with the same type and value. If you have an electrical problem or fuses blow repeatedly, consult an electrician. Do not attempt to dismantle or repair any electrical elements of the machine unless you are competent to do so. If you use cutting fluid of any kind, take great care to make sure it goes nowhere near the motor, control box or wiring harness. Finally, some mini-lathes do not have a seal around the leadscrew. This allows swarf to potentially worm its way into the control box, with disastrous results. I have first-hand experience of this happening.

## Guards

Older mini-lathes are equipped with tiny guards that serve little practical purpose as

*Fig. 2.1 If things start to go wrong, hit the emergency stop.*

Fig. 2.3 The guards on early mini-lathes left something to be desired.

Fig. 2.4 Newer machines have more effective guards.

an arm fixed to a weighted or magnetic base. This can be cleaned easily and placed so it protects the operator without interfering with the use of the machine.

### Cutting Fluids

It may be a surprise to many but the HSE has found health problems, such as dermatitis, asthma and lung damage, from cutting fluid are one of the biggest hazards associated with lathe use. Most mini-lathe owners are unlikely to use floods of coolant and may do most of their work dry or just use small amounts of neat cutting oil applied with a brush or dribbled on to the work. This is less hazardous but it can still get thrown around or give off unpleasant fumes when the work gets hot. Take care to make sure you don't breathe in fumes or overspray, and consider using barrier cream and/or a facemask.

### Gloves and Loose Clothing

Do not wear gloves when working with a machine such as a lathe. If pulled into a moving machine they can lead to terrible injuries. I don't suppose these days many of us would consider wearing a tie in the workshop but beware loose clothing and keep long hair tied back. A more modern hazard is the drawstrings found on hoodies – they can dangle right over the work as you lean forward for a closer look. The best workshop clothing is an overall with a Velcro fastening. Similarly, don't use rags near moving work – kitchen roll is much better as, if caught, it will rip.

### Lighting

It's always important to ensure the lathe and work area is well lit. Ideally, use low voltage lighting or ensure any luminaires are proofed against the entry of swarf or liquids. Avoid old-fashioned fluorescent lights that can give the impression the lathe is not rotating

they rarely offer real protection in the actual working area and in some cases limit the usability of the machine (Fig. 2.3). A guard that interferes in this way gets left open or removed and is therefore pointless. The better and more recent models of mini-

lathe have better designed, curved guards that are wired to an interlock switch (Fig. 2.4).

I have found the easiest and most effective guard is a sheet of polycarbonate about 200–250mm (8–10in) square mounted on

Fig. 2.5 Ear protectors are more comfortable than ear plugs.

if the machine speed synchronizes with the mains frequency. Twelve-volt, LED-based, lights are becoming increasingly popular with machinists.

## Noise

Unlike many machines, a lathe is generally relatively quiet and if it is noisy it is probably trying to tell you things aren't right. For example, a cut may be too heavy, causing shrieking chatter, or an interrupted cut is being taken too quickly or aggressively. There may be times, however, when you can't stop a loud or unpleasant sound from a particular tool due to some resonance or other. You can keep a pair of ear protectors handy but a pack of earplugs are cheaper and equally effective (Fig. 2.5). Do take care though – it's easy to be caught unaware by someone entering the workshop when you are wearing earplugs.

## Tidiness

I live in the real world where workshops are not kept like operating theatres but that does not mean it is sensible to operate a lathe in the midst of chaos. Make sure there is plenty of space for you to move around – specifically that there are no trip hazards waiting to catch you when your attention is on the machine. Keep wires and other tools out of the working area and try to avoid anything that might tempt you to lean over a moving machine.

## Pets and Children

Like a movie actor, beware of working with pets and children! The reasons are obvious. I don't suggest that responsible youngsters should not be allowed in the workshop but do make sure they are properly supervised at all times. Take extra care for their safety and ensure any task you give them is within their capabilities.

## SOME DOS AND DON'TS

**Do** turn the lathe by hand to make sure there are no clashes before starting up.

**Do** make sure work is held securely and the cuts and feeds you use are within the safe capacity of the machine.

**Do** check the engagement and direction of the change gears are what you expect – nothing is worse than turning on and seeing the saddle unexpectedly start moving the wrong way!

**Do** give machining your full attention and avoid distractions in the workshop. You won't do good work if you can't focus on it and the majority of accidents are due to inattention.

**Do** remember you aren't the only person who may walk into your workshop and switch on the power, so make sure things are left in a safe state.

**Do** use eye protection and suitable guards.

**Don't**, ever, leave chuck keys in the chuck.

**Don't** leave the lathe switched on when setting up work or changing tools.

**Don't** try to remove swarf by hand. It is sharp and can easily cut or pull fingers into the work. Keep a bit of wire coat hanger with an 'L' on the end handy for use as a swarf 'puller and poker'.

**Don't** make electrical modifications or repairs unless you have the skills and experience required.

**Don't** leave an unattended machine switched on.

Finally, remember the old adage that you could tell how experienced a machinist was by how many fingers he had lost. Safety is ultimately just common sense and your eyes, ears and fingers are your most valuable assets so take the same care of them as you would any other irreplaceable tool.

# 3    *What is a Mini-lathe?*

In recent years, the availability of relatively inexpensive machine tools of Far Eastern manufacture has created an alternative to second-hand machines as a way into model engineering for those on a budget. If you have bought this book, you may already have invested in a mini-lathe or you may be considering buying your first. You may even have a larger or smaller machine and be considering a mini-lathe as a response to changes in your personal circumstances or requirements.

Mini-lathe seems to have become the accepted description for a range of 3.5in centre height lathes, inexpensive and of Far Eastern manufacture (Fig. 3.1). Personally, I dislike the term as it suggests something toy-like; 'compact-lathe' would be a fairer description as they fit a lot into a small space. Indeed, a long bed mini-lathe has the same centre height as a Myford Super 7 and takes only 3in less between centres, although it does not have a gap bed. The term 'mini-lathe' has, however, become common currency and there is no point trying to coin a different name!

Fifty or sixty years ago, if you could not afford a large, full-featured lathe one choice you had was a tiny lathe such as the Adept, Flexspeed or Centrix Micro – each of which could truly be described as 'mini' and lacked any screwcutting capability (Fig. 3.2). Despite their simplicity, and sometimes crudity, these lathes enabled thousands of people to enter the hobby. Although basic, they were capable of producing good results in skilled hands and those of some owners were modified to become full featured and true precision instruments.

The modern mini-lathe is technically far advanced compared with these historic examples, though it fills a similar niche – meeting the needs of beginners on a limited budget. It has much greater capacity, a built-in variable-speed motor, screwcutting and fine feed, is far more rigid and, with the benefit of modern mass production, is more accurate. Do not make the mistake of assuming these lathes are the machine tool equivalent of the cheap and cheerful tools that often disappoint. Mini-lathes are the small end of a range of industrial machines, not toys, and are capable of almost any model engineering task within their capacity. Indeed, they were originally marketed at well over twice the current price and the only downgrading has been a change from roller to ball bearings in the headstock; a change that can be reversed for the price of a night in the pub.

In the UK, popular models are the SIEG C3 Mini-lathe, Chester Conquest, Clarke CL300M (available from several suppliers including Machine Mart), Axminster SC2 and Warco Mini-Lathe, among others (Fig. 3.3). In the United States there are several further variations. They are all produced to the same basic design by a number of companies in China, notably SIEG, although there are detail differences. You may encounter some even smaller lathes, such as the C0 'baby' lathe, that have a clear family resemblance to mini-lathes (Fig 3.4). Be aware that, although these small machines can be

*Fig. 3.1 The SIEG Super C3 from Arc Euro Trade.*

just what some users want, the true 'mini-lathe' as described in this book is, generally speaking, the smallest lathe with both the capacity and flexibility that most beginners in hobby engineering will need.

There are larger machines of similar design, such as the Chester DB8VS (Fig. 3.5). While these differ in detail, the extra capacity they offer may well appeal to you if you want to tackle larger projects.

All mini-lathes are fundamentally solidly and accurately built and, while they may lack some features, within the limits of their capacity they are capable of producing first class results. Some suppliers retain inspectors to oversee production in China, others inspect and set up the lathes in the UK. All the above models are available from companies with a sound track record of supporting and understanding the needs of model engineers. Buy from such a reputable dealer and you can expect a machine in good order and the same after sales service as if you had bought a machine costing ten times as much.

Some of the optional extras available are:

◆ Digital readouts on the cross slide and top slide
◆ Built-in tachometer (speed readout)
◆ Quick-change toolpost
◆ Lever-operated tailstock.

None of these facilities is essential. A hundred years (or fewer) ago, most model engineers had treadle lathes and did not even possess a three-jaw chuck, yet this did not prevent the achievement of remarkable results! If you can afford just one of these options, choose the lever-operated tailstock. It is the one extra you will use all the time and it will make many repetitive tasks far quicker. Even so, this is an accessory you can add later at minimal cost.

Mini-lathes have a centre height of just over 3.5in (~90mm) (described as a swing of 7in in the US) and, normally, a gap between centres of 12in (305mm). A few machines

Fig. 3.2 Far less sophisticated, the Super Adept was the 'mini-lathe' of its day.

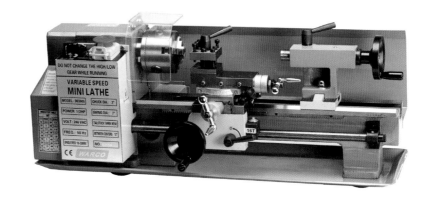

Fig. 3.3 The Warco Mini-lathe is a typical example.

Fig. 3.4 The SIEG C0 is from Axminster. It is much more compact and suited to those who want a smaller lathe to complement another hobby.

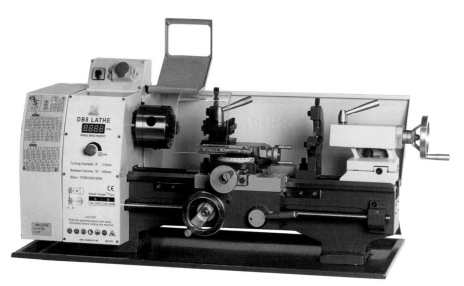

*Fig. 3.5 The Chester DB8VS might suit those seeking something rather larger than a mini-lathe.*

have 10in (254mm) between centres; some machines have 14in (355mm) or even 16in (406mm). Once you fit a chuck or have a long tool in the tailstock this difference is significant and the increase in rigidity with a shorter bed is not significant. I would always recommend getting the largest size compatible with the space you have. The headstock mandrel has a bore of 20mm or just over ¾in. The lathe does not have a gap bed.

These dimensions define the size of work the lathe can tackle. The lack of a gap bed is the main disadvantage compared with more expensive machines. If you are a member of a club or have access to another lathe for the odd job, such as turning a flywheel, then this is no great problem. Otherwise, you are limited to work with a radius of 3.5in, unless you fit a temporary headstock raising block and longer drive belt.

While there is a good range of accessories marketed for mini-lathes, do not assume you are restricted to these. Only a few are specific to mini-lathes, such as alternative leadscrews and steadies. Most other accessories for small lathes will fit straight on if purchased in the correct size (such as tools, chucks or centres) or can be easily adapted to fit a mini-lathe (such as quick release toolposts). Mini-lathes have a number 3 Morse Taper (MT3) in the headstock and MT2 in the tailstock, typical sizes for model engineering lathes. These allow the easy and rapid fitting of a wide range of accessories. Some are made especially for these lathes but, as they are usual sizes for small lathes, there are many generic accessories available new and second-hand.

The usual tool-holder is a four-position model, set at the correct height for ⁵⁄₁₆in tool-bits with little or no packing. Quick release

tool-holders are readily available. The tool-post is mounted on a 360 degree swivelling top slide.

Mini-lathes come with a set of changewheels to allow screwcutting and automatic feed. The leadscrew comes in metric and imperial versions, so buy the version that suits your usual preference for screwcutting. Changing over the leadscrew is not a five-minute job but, as we will see, there is an easy alternative.

My choice was a CL300M that had been returned, hardly used, and this is the machine generally featured in this book. Don't take this to mean the CL300M is better or worse than any other model – I just saw it going cheap and made a snap decision! Having been not been changed significantly since 1998, it does have a lower spec than more recent variants.

It was soon apparent that several standard accessories were missing, including the chuck key and several changewheels, but these were forwarded rapidly and without question. Due to my inexperience, it took me longer to realize that, although without visible wear or damage (the chuck was dated the year before I bought the machine), the lathe was not very well set up. I have since discovered the remedies to a few problems caused by my own inexperience. Along the way I have been pleasantly surprised – while some aspects of the lathe are rather basic (such as the crude bolt to fix the tailstock), it is rigid, accurate and reliable. I cannot guarantee every single point I cover applies to all other mini-lathes but, by the same token, the general principles will apply to any small lathe of similar size.

# 4   *Choosing a Mini-Lathe*

When looking at various models of mini-lathe you will be struck by the many versions of the 'same' model available. Mini-lathes come out of a number of factories in China and each supplies many importers around the world. The most common are those made by SIEG in Shanghai – the C2, C3 and Super C3 – but these are often 'badge engineered' and painted in the colours of the importer (Figs 4.1, 4.2 and 4.3). Others are made by concerns such as Real Bull but all have their roots in the same original design. In the UK importers include Chester with its off-white Conquest, Warco's Mini-Lathe in their house green, Clarke's signal yellow CL300M, Arc Euro Trade's machines in SIEG maroon and Axminster in white and aqua. In the United States there are several further variations, notably from Grizzly (green) and Harbor Freight, again in SIEG factory colours. Aussie has started importing SIEG lathes into Australia. There are many other importers in the UK and around the world.

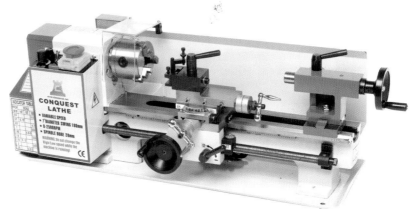

*Fig. 4.1 Chester's version of the mini-lathe is called the Conquest.*

*Fig. 4.2 The Clarke CL300M is sold by Machine-Mart and some other suppliers.*

Although they are all produced to the same basic design as described in the previous chapter, there are detail differences, from built-in tachometers to the quality of the set-up. All these machines are fundamentally built solidly and accurately and, while they may lack some features, within the limits of their capacity they are capable of producing first class results. Don't be dazzled by this rainbow of colours. If you decide to buy a mini-lathe, I suggest you do two things: First, decide what specification you want and, second, find a supplier with whom you feel comfortable who sells a machine to that spec. Buy from

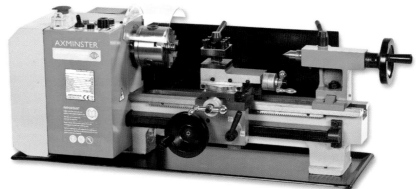

*Fig. 4.3 The SC2 is a well specified mini-lathe from Axminster.*

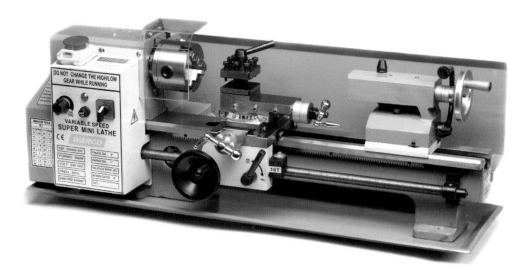

*Fig. 4.4 Warco's Super Mini-lathe has a longer bed than its standard machine.*

a reputable dealer who specifically serves hobby engineers and be confident you will get the same sales service as if you had bought a relatively huge machine costing much more.

Some machines are marketed by the same company at different levels of specification. For example, Warco's Super Mini-lathe is 350mm between centres – 50mm longer than the standard machine. It has a brushed 550w motor – 150w more powerful than their standard machine – and it has a digital rev counter fitted (Fig. 4.4). The Super Mini-lathe's tailstock features an over-centre,

cam-operated lock that is easier to use than the standard spanner and nut adjustment. The tailstock base is also twice the length, thereby allowing for greater stability.

Another choice you will find is between the C3-type machines, with a brushed DC motor and a geared spindle, and the Super C3 machines, which have a brushless DC motor of greater power output (Fig. 4.5). The C2 was an earlier version with a shorter bed and less powerful brushed motor. For all this variety, the fundamental dimensions and operation of all the different types of mini-lathes are essentially similar.

## OPTIONS

Let's run through the main options from which you may need to choose when buying your lathe.

As mentioned before, I would suggest going for as long a bed as you can obtain. Some suppliers may offer an induction hardened bed. This may appeal if you expect your lathe to enjoy a particularly long and hardworking life but should not be seen as a necessity for normal use.

Hardened bedways will extend the life of your lathe before the bed needs to be reground. The amount of hardening that can be applied to a cast iron bed is limited. Mine has unhardened ways and has had a fairly typical sixteen years' hobby use yet shows no signs of needing a regrind. I would suggest this is a 'nice to have' but not essential.

The metric leadscrew option is of greatest importance to those who wish to cut screw threads. It is possible to swap between metric and imperial leadscrews (and half nuts) but, as we will see, metric threads can be cut on imperial machines, and vice versa.

Digital readouts are a point of debate. With the handle-type fitted to a mini-lathe they do not solve issues of backlash but nonetheless some users find them invaluable. They can be retrofitted. A built in

*Fig. 4.5 The Super C3 combines a long bed and brushless motor.*

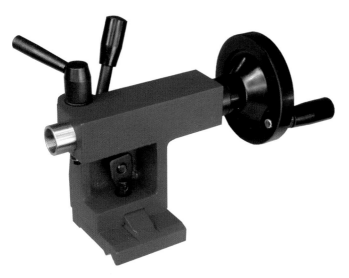

*Fig. 4.6 A lever-locking tailstock is a great time-saver.*

◆ Change wheels for screwcutting
◆ Allen keys
◆ Spanners
◆ Four-way toolpost
◆ Tailstock centre

A set of cutting tools and sometimes other accessories may also be included. We will revisit all these items in more detail as we get to know the lathe in later chapters.

Other accessories you may see marketed as being for your choice of mini-lathe include:

◆ MT2 tailstock drill chuck
◆ MT2 rotating centre
◆ 80mm four-jaw independent chuck
◆ Faceplate
◆ MT3 centre
◆ Fixed steady (rest)
◆ Travelling (or follow) steady (rest)
◆ Metric/imperial leadscrew conversion set

tachometer (speed readout) is useful at the beginning but as you get more confident you will ignore the tacho and listen to the 'cut' instead.

A lever locking tailstock is a very convenient accessory, though it is not essential and can be fitted as an aftermarket upgrade (Fig. 4.6).

The option of a brushless motor is a good idea, especially if you hope to work the lathe quite hard. But, unlike a locking tailstock, it is not an easy retro fit. This is not just as a new controller board is needed as well but because the bed castings are different to accommodate the larger motor. That said, nothing is impossible.

None of these facilities are essential. A hundred years ago, many model engineers did not even possess a three-jaw chuck and drove their lathes with a foot-motor (treadle). This did not prevent some achieving work of a standard far higher than I can attain with all my accessories! If you can afford just one of these options, you may wish to choose the lever-operated tailstock, not the high technology readouts. It is the one extra you will use all the time and it will make many repetitive tasks far quicker. Even so, this is an accessory you can add yourself later, either buying a lever tailstock or modifying a bolt-on version.

## ACCESSORIES

Standard accessories that are supplied with most, if not all, mini-lathes are (Fig. 4.7):

◆ 80mm three-jaw self-centring chuck with additional jaws
◆ Chuck key

As you get to know your lathe, you will probably discover a need for many of these, particularly the ones near the top of the list that are almost indispensable. Be aware though that, aside from the faceplate, steadies and the leadscrew sets, these are all standard items that can be sourced from various suppliers.

Indeed, while there is a good range of accessories marketed for mini-lathes, do not assume you are restricted to those on these lists. Most other accessories for small lathes will fit straight on if purchased in the correct size (such as tools, chucks or centres) or can be adapted easily to fit a mini-lathe (such as a quick release toolpost). Mini-lathes have a number 3 Morse Taper (MT3) in the headstock and MT2 in the tailstock, typical sizes for model engineering lathes. These allow the easy and rapid fitting of a wide range of accessories. Some are made especially for these lathes but as they are the usual sizes for small lathes there are many generic accessories available new

*Fig. 4.7 Typical accessories for a mini-lathe (three-jaw chuck not shown).*

and second-hand. As for chucks, there are many sources of 80mm bolt-on chucks but check they have the appropriate register to fit the spigot (usually 63mm) of your lathe's spindle. Larger chucks can be fitted but you may have to machine a suitable backplate.

## CUTTING TOOLS

The standard mini-lathe tool-holder is a four-position model, set at the correct height for ⁵⁄₁₆in (approximately 8mm) toolbits with little or no packing. Quick release tool-holders are readily available and are a real boon but you don't need one to get started. The toolpost is mounted on a 360 degree swivelling top slide.

There are a number of different sets of tooling sold as 'compatible' with mini-lathes but any tool with a ⁵⁄₁₆in or smaller shank can be used. High speed steel (HSS) tools (ground from a single piece of silver-coloured high-speed steel) are a good place to start. Treat brightly-coloured sets of carbide-tipped tools with caution. Tipped tooling that works well with smaller, low-powered lathes needs care in the choosing as most carbide is meant for peeling huge, hot chips with powerful machines worked hard. We will look at this later. A set of five or six HSS tools of different shapes will get you off to a good start (Fig. 4.8). Some mini-

*Fig. 4.8 A set of pre-ground HSS tools are a great help when getting started.*

lathes come with, or have available as a standard accessory, a set of tools, the most useful of which are a set of 6mm square double-ended tools and holder that ensures they are at the correct height.

To conclude, choosing a lathe is not an ordinary purchase. This machine could be the heart of your hobby for many years to come so take your time and enjoy the process of choosing and acquiring it. Make sure you also get at least a basic set of HSS tools. If you can obtain some aluminium alloy or 'free cutting mild steel' bar of about 25mm (1in) diameter at the same time, then you will have something to 'practise on' when you start cutting metal!

# 5 Getting to Know the Lathe

On close inspection, the mini-lathe is a surprisingly complex bit of equipment, sprouting levers and handwheels in all directions, a gearbox and multiple moving parts (Fig. 5.1). There may be a temptation to dive straight in but most new owners will agree it is worth getting to know what's what first. In this section we will mostly be looking in detail at an Arc Euro Trade Super C3 lathe and its accessories but any major differences from other types of mini-lathe will be pointed out.

At its simplest, a lathe consists of a bed with two pointed centres, between which the work is rotated. Some form of rest or toolholder is attached to the bed so suitable tools can be applied to the work to remove material in a controlled way. The simplest metalworking lathes, the 'watchmaker's turns', are literally just this, a pair of opposed points fitted to a bar, and a toolrest – the work is rotated by pulling a cord wrapped around it back and forth. Like most metalworking lathes, mini-lathes are considerably more sophisticated than 'turns' but the basic construction of bed, headstock, tailstock and tool-support is there, just with many added features.

This chapter will look at the functions of the various parts of the lathe. Later chapters will look in more detail at setting up and adjusting these parts, as well as use of the machine. Fig. 5.2 shows an exploded diagram of a SIEG C3 mini-lathe. All mini-lathes have similar construction, although Super C3 lathes do not have a gearbox inside the headstock.

## THE BED

The bed of mini-lathes is a substantial iron casting, ground in the 'American' style with an inverted-V along the front (Fig. 5.3). This raised section ensures the accurate alignment of the headstock, saddle and tailstock, and any other accessories fitted to the bed, such as steadies or stops. The underside of the front and back shears of the bed and its top surface are also finished accurately. A central slot allows for the attachment of the tailstock or fixed steadies

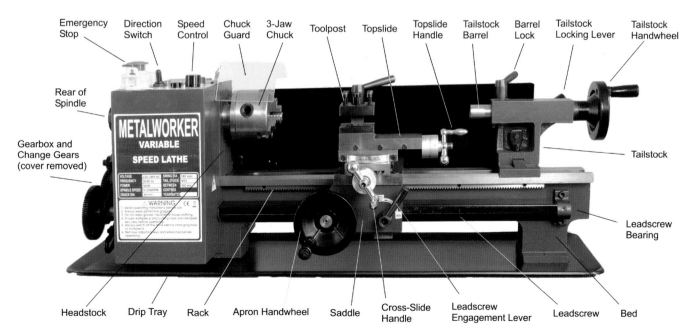

*Fig. 5.1 The main parts of a mini-lathe.*

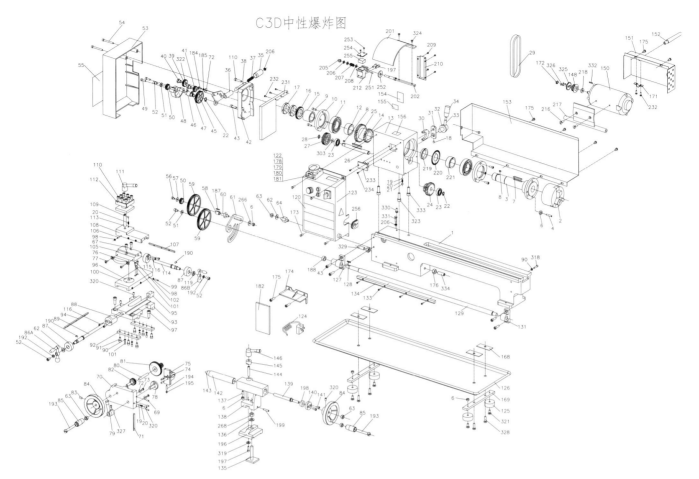

Fig. 5.2 An exploded diagram of a standard C3 (courtesy SIEG).

*Fig. 5.3 The bed of a long-bed mini-lathe.*

16in bed version relies on the tailstock over-hanging the end of the bed by ½in to achieve its specified capacity and if the same is done on my own, nominally 300mm (12in) capac-ity, lathe it will actually take work comfort-ably more than 13in long. These figures are also complicated by the actual overhang of the centres used. In practice, most turning is done with the chuck fitted and a rotat-ing tailstock centre, which will reduce the capacity by 75mm (3in) or more.

**Serial Numbers**

The serial numbers of lathes made by SIEG are normally to be found on top of the rear right hand corner of the bed. The method of stamping can raise the metal around the numbers and you may wish to lightly

but it is usually not highly finished as its purpose is just to provide a secure fixing for these fittings, not alignment.

The bed length is defined as the largest length of workpiece that can be turned in the lathe (rather than the overall length of the machine). They are usually quoted in imperial units and different machines may be obtained with 10in (254mm), 12in (305mm), 14in (355mm) and 16in (406mm) bed lengths. The 10in bed length machines are distinctly cramped compared with the larger versions but these figures are not as clear-cut as you may suppose. Micro-Mark's

*Fig. 5.4 Serial numbers are usually stamped at the end of the rear shear of the bed.*

dress the area around the figures level to ensure the tailstock is not slightly pushed out of alignment when moved to the end of the bed. As is often the case, more recent machines appear to have this done more neatly (Fig. 5.4).

## LEADSCREW

Along the front of the bed is a long, accurate screw with an Acme-form thread, either 1.5mm pitch or 16 threads per inch (Fig. 5.5). The pitch of the leadscrew is the sole material difference between most metric and imperial mini-lathes. By using different change gears in the headstock gearbox the leadscrew can be driven at different speeds for thread cutting or automatic feed. Naturally, on an imperial lathe it is easier to cut imperial size threads and metric threads on a metric machine but universal thread cutting is not a problem, as we shall see

*Fig. 5.5 The leadscrew of this imperial mini-lathe is sixteen threads per inch.*

later. There are oiling points at each end of the leadscrew.

## MOTOR

At the rear left of the bed is the motor, usually hidden behind a sheet metal guard (Fig. 5.6). This can be either a brushed or brushless motor, with the brushless motors being favoured for flexibility and robustness. The brushless motors are slightly longer and so the beds of the more recent brushless motor lathes are subtly different, and brushed motor lathes cannot easily be converted to brushless.

*Fig. 5.6 A metal cover protects the brushless motor of an SC3.*

## HEADSTOCK

At the left end of the bed, with the control box attached to its front, is the headstock (Fig. 5.7). Following modern practice, this is basically a rigid cast iron box, fitted accurately to the inverted V and with bearings pressed in at each end for the spindle, which is driven by the motor attached to the back of the bed. Most mini-lathes are supplied with deep groove ball bearings. A popular upgrade is to replace the original bearings with roller bearings or angular contact ball bearings. This generally improves the surface finish obtainable and reduces chatter, especially for demanding tasks such as form cutting and parting off. These bearings are greased and should not need regular re-lubrication, unlike some lathes.

*Fig. 5.7 The headstock of a much-modified CL300M.*

Mini-lathes with brushed motors have a simple gearbox arrangement within the headstock, operated by a lever at the back (Fig. 5.8). High gear is roughly twice the speed of low gear, and therefore has less torque. It is possible to damage these gears by changing them with the lathe running or if you have a big 'smash up', such as running a cutter into a chuck. They can be replaced. Metal gears are available but are noisier and the danger with them is any accident causes less easily rectified damage elsewhere. In order to keep the motor running cool, it is best to operate in low gear unless really high speed running is required. Mini-lathes with the more flexible brushless DC motors do not require these gears.

At the left hand end of the headstock is a gearbox cover with a hole to allow easy access to the end of the spindle bore. The cover is held in place by two cap screws. This can be removed to change the leadscrew

*Fig. 5.8 A simple gearbox in the headstock is operated by the high/low lever, which should only be used when the machine is stationary.*

Fig. 5.9 The tumbler reverse lever can be difficult to reach.

Fig. 5.10 A mini-lathe spindle is a solid and well-machined component.

Fig. 5.12 The tailstock barrel is graduated to assist with drilling holes to depth.

gearing for screwcutting. It is notched at the back for the 'tumbler reverse' lever. This lever changes the direction the leadscrew rotates relative to the spindle, and therefore the direction the saddle moves when auto feed is engaged (Fig. 5.9). Removing and replacing the gearbox cover is a tedious operation, creating the temptation to leave it off, with the resulting risk of things (and fingers) being pulled into the gears. A very simple modification for a lift-on/lift-off cover is detailed later.

## SPINDLE

As mentioned, the function of the headstock is to provide a solid support for the spindle (Fig. 5.10). The business end of the spindle is at the right hand end of the headstock. It has two ways of mounting accessories. The spindle is bored through to allow work up to 19mm (¾in) diameter to pass through it but at the end is opened out into a number three Morse taper (MT3) socket. Tooling and accessories to fit this standard taper are widely available – note that *any* accessory with an MT3 taper can potentially be used here, it does not have to be made specifically for a mini-lathe. Examples of MT3 accessories include the dead centre typically supplied with the machine and items such as collet chucks, boring heads, drills, reamers and even MT3 collets that fit directly into the spindle. With many types of accessory, it is wise to use a drawbar through the spindle

to hold the taper securely in place. We will revisit this later when we look at accessories in more detail.

The other mounting arrangement is the flange, to which items such as chucks and faceplates can be attached by nuts and three or four M6 studs. This flange is specific to mini-lathes and is 80mm in diameter with a short 55mm register. Usually the lathe comes with a faceplate and an 80mm three-jaw chuck that fit directly to this flange. Other 80mm three and four-jaw chucks and ER collet chucks can be obtained to fit these flanges but if you want to use a larger chuck (a 100mm chuck is a popular choice) you will have to fit an intermediate adaptor or 'backplate'. This is not unusual and many lathes require such a fitting to be used for all chucks. We will look at fitting a backplate later.

## TAILSTOCK

Opposed to the headstock is the tailstock (Fig. 5.11), also aligned on the inverted V of

the bed. Instead of a rotating spindle, this has a sliding barrel with a smaller number 2 Morse taper (MT2) socket, which can be 'wound' in and out with a handwheel. Again, MT2 is an industrial standard and a vast number of accessories to fit the tailstock can be obtained easily. On top of the tailstock is a short lever used to lock the barrel in position. The tailstock barrel is graduated; on my elderly machine this scale is virtually unreadable but, as with so many aspects of newer mini-lathes, the standard of the graduations has been improved greatly (Fig. 5.12). The barrel lock uses a split pinch-nut that minimizes movement of the barrel and operates typically over about a quarter-turn – it does not need excessive force to lock the tailstock. Keep it pinched up for normal operations and just loosen it slightly when drilling from the tailstock.

*Fig. 5.11 The tailstock can support the end of work or carry various tools.*

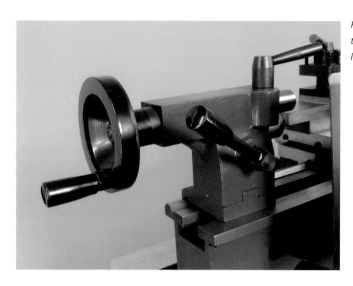

*Fig. 5.13 At the back of the tailstock is the locking lever.*

The tailstock has two main functions – supporting long work and presenting tools (such as drills) along the lathe axis. When used as a support, one typically fits a fixed or revolving centre. Obviously, the relatively short barrel movement is not sufficient on its own, so the tailstock can be slid along the bed and fixed in any convenient position. Older models had bolt-on tailstocks that were rather tedious to move but most of the more recent machines have lever-locking tailstocks, which are a real boon (Fig. 5.13).

Less obviously, it is important the axis of the tailstock barrel can be aligned accurately with that of the spindle for most work, although for some methods of taper turning it needs to be offset. The tailstock is therefore made in two parts, clamped by a pair of screws, and can be adjusted back and forth for alignment. This is something we will review in detail later. The vertical alignment of the tailstock should be more or less 'spot-on' from new.

Unlike the spindle, the tailstock barrel is not hollow right through. Instead it has a 'self-ejecting' arrangement. A criticism of mini-lathes is that the length of the barrel means tanged tooling will self-eject before the barrel is fully retracted. If this is an issue for you, it is usually easy enough to cut the tangs off tooling, although if they are

hardened you may need to use a cut off wheel in a grinder or rotary multi tool.

As the barrel is not drilled right through, a drawbar cannot be fitted. This means, when using a tool in the tailstock, you have to rely on the self-holding properties of the MT2 taper and the pressure of the toolbit against the work. The forces involved should not normally pull the tooling forwards, although brass and bronze can 'grab' a drill when it breaks through and jerk it out of the taper. A bigger risk is that a drill worked too hard can seize in the work and spin the taper. This can result in scoring of the taper

or, even worse, the tailstock socket. Counter intuitively, lightly oiling the taper can help ensure a more secure fit and help avoid this happening. This also helps avoid galling if the taper does spin but the real cure is keeping both the socket and the tapers you fit in it scrupulously clean. A tapered piece of softwood about 6mm (¼in) thick that fits into the socket is a useful aid to removing swarf from any taper socket.

If you do get damage to the socket, it is possible to remove burrs by gently turning an MT2 reamer in it by hand but I don't advise making a habit of this as eventually it will lose its accuracy. Any raised burrs on an external taper should be carefully stoned off, trying to avoid marking the undamaged parts of the surface.

## SADDLE

Between the headstock and tailstock sits the apparatus for presenting tools to the work and moving them to make cuts. As standard, there are three 'slides' arranged one above the other (Fig. 5.14). At the bottom is the saddle, a hefty casting (Fig. 5.15) that slides left to right along the inverted V. At the front of the saddle is the apron, which has a large, geared handwheel that moves

*Fig. 5.14 A profusion of handles sprout from the saddle and slides.*

*Fig. 5.15 The saddle casting is guided by the front 'inverted V'.*

*Fig. 5.16 The cross slide is used to move tools across the bed of the lathe.*

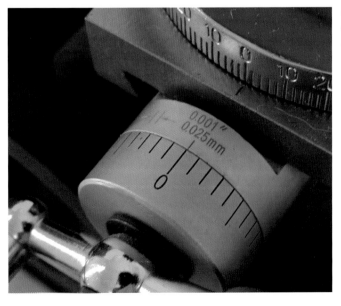

*Fig. 5.17 'Dual reading' adjustable dials are satin finished and easy to read.*

the saddle left or right. It can be used to make a cut and, although it is quite highly geared, many experienced users do so. Take care if doing this as the handwheel is not graduated, making it easy to overshoot.

To the right of the handwheel is the half-nut engagement lever. When held down, this engages a split nut behind the apron with the leadscrew so that, with the change gears set appropriately, it can be moved along under power. For most normal cutting, a very high gear ratio is used to give steady, gradual movement, helping you to get a fine surface finish. *See* the sections on basic turning and screwcutting for more details. Lower gear ratios give more rapid movement and are used for screwcutting. The saddle (and the other slides) should be lubricated at the various places where it bears on the bed, ideally with rather thick slideway oil. However, many users just keep the working surfaces covered with a film of neat cutting oil, dabbed on from time to time.

## CROSS SLIDE

Across the top of the saddle is a broad 'dove-tail' that bears the cross slide, operated by a smaller handwheel fitted to the saddle (Fig. 5.16). The cross slide moves across the width of the bed and in normal turning is used to adjust the depth of cut. One turn of the handwheel moves the cross slide 1mm or almost exactly 0.040in. It has a resettable index with forty divisions, each division being 0.025mm or 0.001in (a thousandth of an inch, universally known as a 'thou', Fig. 5.17). Take care though – if you are reducing the diameter of a part this will reduce by twice the depth of cut (as you take material off both sides of the work). So a cut of, say, 0.10mm reduces the diameter by 0.20mm.

The cross slide can, with the right tool, also be used to apply 'facing' cuts, creating a flat face on the workpiece. It is important to remember the lathe can be used to create flat faces in this way, as well as cylindrical ones.

## TOP SLIDE

Although the cross slide allows accurate in-out movement, the saddle movement does not give us the same degree of control. What do we do if, when facing a workpiece, we need to move the tool left by a small, precise amount? The answer is to use the top slide (Fig. 5.18), mounted on a swivelling attachment to the cross slide and, again, operated by a handwheel graduated in forty 0.025mm (1 thou) divisions. If the top slide is wound right back, two cap screws are revealed. These can be loosened temporarily so the top slide can be rotated, allowing it to be aligned with the axis of the lathe or angled to permit the easy cutting of tapers (Fig. 5.19). Normally, the top slide is aligned parallel to the lathe axis, a difficult task on some lathes but easy on a mini-lathe as all the surfaces of the slides are ground accurately. This means a small engineer's square can be used against the sides of the cross and top slide to align it. Do not rely on the dial on the side of the top slide, marked in degrees for setting critical angles. This is not very accurate and should be used only as a rough guide (Fig. 5.20). For other angles, a protractor can be used instead of a square but for accurate tapers it is usually necessary to take a 'cut and try' approach, which we will look at later.

## TOOL-HOLDER

The pinnacle of this engineering layer cake is the four-way toolpost (Fig. 5.21). This is a square block with a deep slot all round and three clamp screws per side. Loosening the clamp lever allows it to be rotated (there is a 90 degree index ratchet but you can use intermediate positions). Up to four tools can be fitted at one time, although more than two tends to result in tools pointing in awkward directions. The holder is designed so ⁵⁄₁₆in high tools should be at or just below the correct height, allowing minimal packing to be used. In practice, smaller tools can be used with thicker packing.

*Fig. 5.18 The top-slide can rotate to any angle for cutting tapers.*

*Fig. 5.19 Adjustment is a little awkward, requiring the top slide to be fully retracted.*

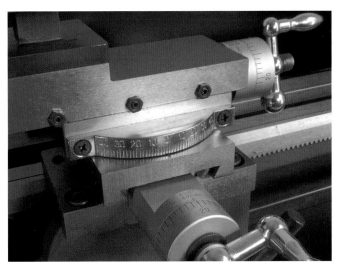

*Fig. 5.20 The top slide angle is only a guide and should not be relied upon for accuracy.*

*Fig. 5.21 The four way toolpost is clamped by an M10 stud.*

## Control Box

We have looked at the main mechanical features of the lathe but before moving on we should go back to the headstock and take a look at the control box (Fig. 5.22). The details vary more between different mini-lathe models than most aspects of these lathes but in general you should find the following controls.

A big red 'emergency stop' switch. In fact, this is a cover for stop and start buttons and is arranged to operate the stop switch if it is pressed. This must be unlocked to allow the lathe to start and, if pressed, the lathe will stop promptly. Make the habit of stopping the lathe with this button, rather than dialling the speed down to zero, so that if and when you need to stop the machine in a hurry you will reach for this switch automatically.

*Fig. 5.22 The controls of an SC3, other models will have detail differences.*

A speed control. To start the lathe, the speed control must be set to zero, then rotated clockwise until the lathe is operating at the desired speed. A no-voltage release arrangement means that once stopped, even if the stop switch is released, the lathe must be deliberately restarted this way. This is a safety feature that also stops the lathe from starting on its own if the supply is interrupted.

With brushed motor lathes the top speed is either about 1,100rpm or 2,200rpm depending on the high/low gear selection. Brushless motor lathes typically have a top speed of about 2,500rpm. The low speed of either type is typically a 'crawl'.

A reversing switch. This allows the lathe to be run backwards. The maximum reverse speed is normally considerably less than the normal maximum forward speed. The bolted flange fixing for chucks means the lathe can be run safely in reverse, although some lathes have screw on chucks and running them this way requires great care. Do not reverse the lathe when it is in motion as this could damage the machine and the back-EMF (electromotive force) generated by the motor could affect the control circuitry.

One or more fuseholders. We will revisit fuses late but for now it suffices to say you should always use fuses of the type and rating specified for your machine. Most lathes also have a power light and some have a second 'fault' light that indicates if the motor protection circuitry has cut in. This usually means the motor has been overloaded, so switch off and let things cool down before proceeding.

On some mini-lathes you will also find a tachometer speed readout or a socket for attaching a remote readout – in the photo this socket has a cover fitted. This uses a detector fitted inside the headstock to read the spindle speed directly. A tachometer often appeals to beginners as they can calculate the 'right' spindle speed for a particular size and type of material from various charts and formulae. In practice, quoted figures usually refer to industrial usage and with smaller machine tools such as mini-lathes different (often lower) speeds, feeds and depths of cut are appropriate. One advantage of variable speed is it is possible to tweak the speed until the machine is cutting well without stress or chatter. The 'feel' for machining developed this way is a valuable skill.

## ACCESSORIES

The number of accessories available to fit a mini-lathe are innumerable and partly this is because so much lathe and general engineering tooling is pretty much generic. In this section, we will just look at the accessories likely to be supplied with the machine or marketed specifically for it.

### 80mm Three-Jaw Self-Centring Chuck

A three-jaw chuck is the most common standard accessory for any small lathe. This is not because it is the best method of work holding but it is far and away the most convenient, especially for the beginner. In essence, it is a rotating vice whose jaws are moved in and out in unison so they hold circular work more or less centrally (Fig. 5.23).

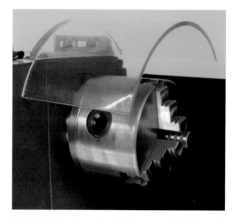

*Fig. 5.23 A three-jaw chuck is the most straightforward method of work holding.*

The chuck is held to the front of the spindle by three nutted studs but relies on a raised register for its accuracy – make sure this is clean before fitting the chuck. Although the chuck is described as 'self-centring', be aware that even expensive three-jaw chucks costing as much as a mini-lathe are not perfect. Your chuck will hold things reasonably concentrically but not perfectly. The chuck should be accompanied by a T-handled key for tightening and loosening the jaws, and a second set of 'outside' jaws for holding work of a larger diameter.

**Change Wheels**

To set up the lathe for screw cutting or fine feed, various trains of change wheels need to be set up in the gearbox (Fig. 5.24). You should find an assortment of gear wheels with the lathe. The standard set for a metric lathe is: 2 × 20, 30, 35, 2 × 40, 45, 50, 60 and 2 × 80. For an imperial lathe the set is rather larger: 2 × 20, 30, 35, 2 × 40, 2 × 45, 2 × 45, 50, 55, 57, 60, 65 and 2 × 80. This is because of the wider range of pitches of imperial threads. As supplied, all but the two twenty-tooth gears will be in nylon. These are surprisingly durable and reasonably quiet but sets of metal change wheels are available as a deluxe accessory.

**Tool Kit**

You should find a spanner or two with the lathe and the smaller of these is for changing gear wheels and adjusting the gib strips. The larger is for releasing the tailstock or removing the handwheels. You may also be given a number of Allen (hex) keys, used for dismantling and adjusting various different parts of the lathe.

You probably won't find a C-spanner for adjusting the headstock bearings in the toolkit. It is worth getting hold of one, or ideally two, if you can. They are available from some of the larger suppliers of mini-lathes.

*Fig. 5.24 These gears are set up to provide a fine feed, rather than for screwcutting.*

**Tailstock Centre**

This is just a short tapered piece of hardened steel that fits snugly in the tailstock, with a sharper 60-degree taper on the other end (Fig. 5.25). It is used to support work with a matching hole (confusingly also known as a 'centre') in it.

*Fig. 5.25 An MT2 plain centre.*

If you are lucky, you may also get some of the following items with your machine, either as standard accessories or as part of a 'bundle deal':

**Cutting Tools**

Naturally, a selection of tools is essential to use the lathe. We will look at these in more detail in the chapter on turning.

**MT2 Tailstock Drill Chuck**

A very common requirement is to drill or ream holes in the centre of work held in the chuck or on a faceplate. A tailstock-fitted chuck is a flexible solution to holding the tools needed for such work (Fig. 5.26). Keyed chucks are perfectly acceptable and a quality keyless chuck is good.

*Fig. 5.26 Tailstock drill chucks are an indispensable accessory.*

## MT2 Rotating Centre

The plain centre supplied with most lathes has a built-in problem – as it does not rotate it needs lubrication of the hole it fits in and even with this it can overheat and damage or wear the work (or itself). The solution (at the expense of a small loss of accuracy) is a rotating centre, which contains accurate bearings and can be used without lubrication and to hold the work rather more firmly than a plain centre.

## 80mm Four-Jaw Independent Chuck

An 80mm four-jaw chuck is a valuable accessory for dealing with difficult or specialized work holding (Fig. 5.27). In contrast to self-centring chucks, independent chucks have individually adjustable jaws. This makes them rather fiddly to use but they often offer a firmer grip. Aided by a suitable indicator device, it is possible to set work to run as truly as you are ever likely to need using one and this is handy if you have round work and want to turn surfaces that are perfectly concentric with the existing diameter. The other, more obvious, advantages of such a chuck is the independent jaws can be used

*Fig. 5.27 Sooner or later you will find yourself needing a four-jaw independent chuck.*

to grip all sorts of shapes and also to align them so any convenient point is on the axis of the lathe. An example of this would be turning an offset round boss on one end of a rectangular bar.

Four-jaw chucks to fit straight on to mini-lathes are readily available but not all 80mm chucks are a direct fit, so tell your supplier what machine it is for when purchasing.

## Faceplate

The faceplate (Fig. 5.28) is an underrated accessory. Much bigger than a chuck, it provides a large and solid base on which work of all sorts and shapes can be attached, once you have got the hang of locating and clamping workpieces securely. They are particularly useful for turning the rims and faces of large spoked flywheels or locomotive wheels.

*Fig. 5.28 A faceplate will help you with working on very large or awkwardly shaped items.*

## MT3 Centre

An MT3 centre is just a larger version of the tailstock centre that will fit in the lathe spindle. It is used chiefly for turning between centres, an approach that supports the work on centre holes drilled in each end. This technique is described in more detail later.

They may be fully hardened or may be tempered so they can be 'skimmed' to provide a perfectly concentric centre, a common requirement with cheaper old

lathes whose spindle bore might not have been aligned perfectly.

## Fixed Steady

A fixed steady is a special support used with work that would otherwise overhang too far from the chuck and that can't be supported from the tailstock – or perhaps to allow a centre hole to be drilled in the end (Fig. 5.29). The standard mini-lathe fixed steady clamps anywhere along the bed and locates on the raised V-guide. It has three bronze 'fingers' that can be adjusted individually so the work runs true.

*Fig. 5.29 A fixed steady is used to support long, overhung work.*

## Travelling (or Follow) Steady

A travelling steady (Fig. 5.30), as its name implies, is fixed to the saddle so it travels back and forth along the bed of the lathe with the tool. Its function is rather different from the fixed steady because it has just two adjustable fingers that are used to stop thin, flexible workpieces from 'riding' on the tip of the tool.

*Fig. 5.30 Travelling steadies provide support to thin, flexible workpieces.*

## Metric/Imperial Leadscrew Conversion Set

It is possible to buy both metric and imperial leadscrews and the various components that work with them to convert a mini-lathe from one type to the other. If you have a metric mini-lathe, you will also need to buy several spare change gears if you want to cut a full range of imperial gears. An alternative, if you just want to cut a few screw threads of the 'other' type, is to invest in a sixty-three tooth conversion gear.

## THE DRIVE TRAIN

There are two basic types of motor fitted to mini-lathes – brushed and brushless DC. They are very different beasts, so let's take them in turn. Brushed motors are the 'traditional' type that use solid carbon blocks (the brushes) running against copper segments (the commutator) to send current through the many different motor windings in turn. Brushless motors are recent technology for small lathes, made possible by the development of rapid, efficient ways of switching high-power electric current. They have a permanent magnet on the shaft instead of a wound armature. There are three windings in the motor body and current is switched between them electronically.

### Brushed DC Motors

Originally, all mini-lathes had brushed DC motors, and even today 350-watt brushed motors are fitted to the majority of machines (Fig. 5.31). The high torque generated by the drive circuitry of a standard mini-lathe does a good job of keeping a steady motor speed when running slowly on heavy loads. This creates the illusion the machine can cope with jobs strictly beyond its capability, or at least that of the motor. Long, slow jobs with heavy cuts can easily overheat the motor owing to the reliance on a fan on the armature for cooling, which is ineffective at slow speeds. One modification is to fit a 12v computer fan to the back of the motor, arranged to assist the built-in fan during normal running. A criticism of this idea is that the external fan could 'compete' with the built-in fan if the lathe is run at high speed in reverse – but how often does one run the lathe flat out in reverse?

A feature of many lathes fitted with single-speed motors is back-gear, usually providing a 4:1 or 6:1 reduction in speed with a complementary increase in torque. This is clearly a benefit on a machine that may otherwise have only three speeds within a relatively narrow range. Mini-lathes, with their variable speed, have less need for such a feature but the high/low gear selector behind the headstock is a 'back gear' of sorts and offers an approximate 2:1 reduction, the motor drive belt running to a shaft below the main spindle of the machine. This does give some useful extra 'grunt' at low speeds and has the benefit of keeping up the motor revs. Indeed, motor cooling is much more effective when the motor runs faster, so if you have a brushed motor on your lathe it is a good idea to always run it in low gear, aside from when you need high speed.

If you have been working your lathe too hard you may discover it starts to run roughly, especially at low speeds. This is a symptom of one of the many windings in the motor burning out. It is still possible for current to flow but at some points in the motor's rotation it will have to travel 'the long way round', causing the uneven running. You may get away with using a motor in this condition but this is a clear signal it will fail completely sooner or later and continuing to use it may burn out the controller board.

Should you have the misfortune to overheat the motor and it burns out completely, you have little option other than to source a replacement. If you find a second-hand replacement, try to make sure it really is pristine – it is not unknown for unscrupulous sellers to pass off motors with one burnt out winding as fully working.

Removal and replacement of the motor is straightforward but made much easier if the lathe is placed so you can access it easily from all sides. Switch off and unplug the machine, open the control panel and

*Fig. 5.31 Mini-lathe brushed motors typically have round cases.*

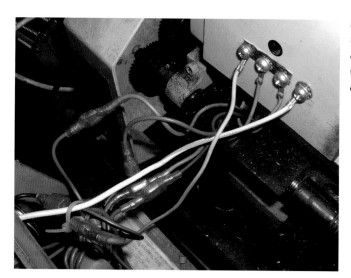

*Fig. 5.32 It is essential these earth connections are replaced after any work on the lathe's electrics.*

disconnect the spade connectors from the motor and its earth connection (Fig. 5.32). Keep a photographic record to help make sure everything goes back in the right place. You can now remove the motor cover and undo the nuts or screws (depending on model) holding the motor in place on the bed, unhook it from the drive belt and lift it free. Replacement of the original or adding a new motor is the reverse of this, except that you will need to fine tune its position to get the drive belt tension correct. This procedure is described in the chapter on setting up the lathe.

Even if you treat your motor with a proper degree of respect, you may still find that, after much use, it starts to run poorly or spark and make 'ozone' smells. These are signs of the carbon brushes wearing out and they should be replaced immediately as poor brushes will damage the commutator and could damage the controller board. It is supposedly possible to change the brushes with the motor in place as there is an access hole in the bed for the brush at the front. Don't waste your time trying to do this because it's quicker to remove the motor.

The brushes are fitted behind two circular screw-plugs in the end cap and comprise the actual carbon brush wired through the middle of a long spring to a contact on the end (Fig. 5.33). You may get away with a

simple swap but if the brushes need changing there is probably a build-up of carbon on the commutator and fully dismantling the motor and carefully cleaning the commutator is required. A wooden toothpick is a nice gentle way to clean any possible shorts between commutator segments. It is rare the commutator on one of these motors is so worn it needs skimming and this is a task that needs great care. The motor armature must be mounted between centres (in another lathe) and a very light cut taken along the commutator with a very sharp tool. The commutator segments then need to be inspected closely and any copper whiskers shorting between segments removed.

*Fig. 5.33 Replacement carbon brushes are inexpensive and easy to fit.*

Mechanical failures of the motors are far rarer than blown windings or worn brushes. If an end cap were to break, it could be replaced with one from a duff motor. The bearings are a standard off-the-shelf size and cheap and easy to source. If the lathe gets noisy or simply fails to turn, even when the motor operates normally, then the high/low gear selector may be not be engaged properly or, worse, the gears may have stripped. *See* the section on the headstock for advice on how to cure this. The best way to avoid this problem is, again, to use low gear whenever possible, never change gear with the lathe operating and always ensure that, whatever gear you are using, the lever is engaged fully.

### Brushless DC Motors

The most recent versions of mini-lathes are fitted with high-powered brushless direct current (BLDC) motors (Fig. 5.34). These are a very different beast to the old brushed motors, requiring more complex control circuitry. They are better suited to low speed running, offering greater torque and smoother operation. One more subtle difference is that the windings of a BLDC motor are in the casing, rather than on the rotor, and this can improve cooling somewhat.

More sophisticated control means BLDC motors can be used satisfactorily over a larger speed range. It is also practical to make more powerful motors of similar size and mini-lathe BLDC motors are typically rated at 500W. For these reasons, mini-lathes with these motors are not fitted with geared headstocks, a simplification that removes a potential source of mechanical failure. This means these lathes have a longer drive belt running directly from the motor to the spindle and a slightly differently shaped mounting plate for the tumbler reverse gears.

It is not unreasonable to assume that, in the event of a brushed motor failing, a BLDC motor would make an excellent upgrade.

*Fig. 5.34 Brushless motors for mini-lathes usually have 'square' casings.*

Unfortunately, although of similar bulk, the BLDC motors are rather longer and require a modified bed casting, so they cannot be fitted in the place of a standard brushed motor. That said, nothing is impossible and the ingenious owner could consider 'hanging' a BLDC motor off the back of the headstock with a countershaft or some other modified drive.

With no brushes to burn out, the most likely failure mode for a brushless motor is a burnt out winding. However, to date there have been few reports of such a failure. It certainly does appear a brushless motor is the power source of choice if you are purchasing a new mini-lathe.

## Motor Controller Boards

Within the control box, you will find the controller board (Fig. 5.35). Treat mini-lathe electrics with extra respect, the motor runs off rectified mains (essentially some 350V direct current). DC shocks are more severe than AC shocks, partly because if you grip a live wire, your grip will tighten on it whereas AC makes you more likely to drop it. So, although you may be used to low voltage DC, that inside a mini-lathe is potentially *more* dangerous than the mains. Unless you really know your electrics, don't go exploring in there and get any problems that arise sorted out by a competent electrician. If you do feel competent to work on the electrics, ensure the lathe is unplugged for several

minutes before opening anything up and leave it unplugged until everything is safely reassembled.

Controlling high voltage DC is tricky because it places big demands on components and, especially in the early days, there were reliability issues with the controller boards. There are now several versions of mini-lathe controller boards in circulation. This is where it can pay to source your lathe from one of the larger suppliers rather than the 'bargain basement' importers as the control board is one of the less visible corners to cut when minimizing the price.

At one time 'Made in the USA' boards were popular. They may have been more reliable once but there no longer appear to be any significant advantages over the Chinese boards. It is now less common for a controller board to burn out but if this does happen

to you replacement boards can be sourced from most mini-lathe suppliers. The controller boards for BLDC motors are particularly robust and relatively few failures have been reported but bear in mind you cannot use BLDC boards with brushed motors or vice versa – they simply won't work.

It is not a hugely difficult task to swap out a damaged controller board, for those experienced in electrical work, but if you have any doubts about your competence to do this ask an expert to do it. The control box is screwed to the front of the headstock. All the connections should be either number-tagged blades that screw to special connectors with matching numbers or blade and receptacle connectors with size and gender chosen to ensure they are connected properly. In the case of the earth connections, they are rings fitted on the end of very obvious green and yellow wires that mount on a series of screws in the front of the headstock.

Even though the connections should be well marked, I suggest keeping a record of what joins to what – a couple of photos on your mobile phone can be very useful for this – and attaching stickers or tags to any unmarked wires. You must make sure you are swapping like for like as there are a number of versions with different connections. If in doubt send a good picture of your damaged board to the

*Fig. 5.35 A typical mini-lathe controller board. If fitting a replacement, ensure it is the right model for your lathe (by permission of SIEG).*

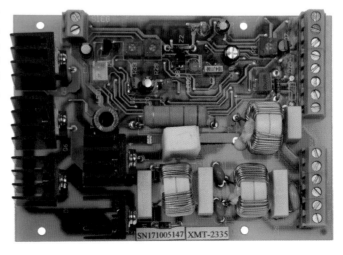

supplier and they will make sure you get a proper replacement.

I make no apologies for repeating the advice to always use 'low' gear unless you want an extra fast cut as this doubles the motor speed, reduces the load and makes more torque available for cutting. Personally, I would rarely use high gear anyway, although it is useful for drilling small holes or finishing small components. Slow running in 'high gear' probably leads to more burnt out mini-lathe motors than any other cause. Make 'low' gear your default.

Using the correct rating of fuse is your best protection against overloading the motor. At least one owner learned the hard way. Frustrated by blowing fuses, they fitted a larger fuse and got away with it for ages.

Then they took on a larger, longer job and blew the motor instead of the fuse. So buy a few packets of 1.6A quick blow fuses. It is easy to damage high-powered electric motors such as those fitted to mini-lathes if they are stalled for any length of time and a packet or three of fuses is a lot cheaper than a new motor. They won't break anyone's bank and, with a proper replacement handy, you won't be tempted to fit a larger fuse.

Some mini-lathes are fitted with an internal circuit breaker as well as a fuse, the operation of which lights a 'fault' indicator (Fig. 5.36). Owners competent with electrical work may consider retrofitting a circuit-breaker to replace the fuse. Bear in mind a breaker trips more slowly than a fuse. It is also critical to get exactly the right rating of

Fig. 5.36 *Some mini-lathes have a fault indicator to show if the machine has been overloaded.*

breaker for your machine; too high a rating and it is useless, too low and the breaker can trip if the motor is run at full speed in high gear for any length of time. Seek the advice of a competent electrician or stick to fuses.

# 6 Setting up the Lathe

## UNPACKING THE LATHE

Some mini-lathes are supplied in colourful cardboard boxes, padded out with expanded polystyrene (Styrofoam) packing. Others are supplied secured to the base of robust wooden packing cases. There are instances of lathes in lighter packaging suffering minor damage, especially to the sheet metal swarf tray. If your lathe arrives by courier, make sure you check the packaging and note any damage before signing for it. Hang on to the packaging until you are sure everything works as it should, just in case you need to return it for attention.

Mini-lathes typically have a gross weight of 40–50kg (88–110lb), depending largely on the length of the bed. Although they are small lathes, this is still a pretty hefty lift, so it is a good idea to have a friend handy to help with moving the machine around.

Once you have opened the crate or box, check the included accessories are all present and in good condition. Bear in mind the included accessories can vary widely between models and suppliers. A new mini-lathe should be supplied with a printed manual. Some of these are better than others but you should read it through carefully, including the safety, electrical and operating instruction sections.

## CLEANING

As you unpack the machine, you will find much of it is covered in a clear preservative coating or a rather thick, red grease (colloquially referred to as chicken fat). This

---

**MINI-LATHE MANUALS ONLINE**

*Some mini-lathe manuals can be downloaded from the internet as pdf files. You may find them useful to refer to, even if you have a different make of machine, but be aware there are detail differences between machines.*

**Arc Euro Trade SC3 Mini-lathe Preparation Guide**
*www.arceurotrade.co.uk/projects/ prepguides/C3%20Mini-Lathe%20 Preparation%20Guide.pdf*

**Axminster SC2 Mini-lathe**
*www.axminster.co.uk/media/ downloads/505102_manual.pdf*

**Clarke CL300M**
*www.m-p.co.uk/muk/acrobat/clarke/ cl300m-instructions.pdf*

**Grizzly G8688**
*https://d27ewrs9ow50op.cloudfront.net/ manuals/g8688_m.pdf*

**Micro-Mark MicroLux 7x16 Mini-lathe**
*www.micromark.com/html_pages/ instructions/84631i/84631lathe.pdf*

*You may find it easier to search for these guides by their titles, rather than typing in the long links!*

---

is not a lubricant but a protection against rust, so it needs to be removed and the lathe properly lubricated. The grease is easily removed with a stiff 25mm (1in) paintbrush and paraffin (kerosene) or a similar gentle organic solvent. Obviously such cleaning should be carried out in a well ventilated area away from sources of ignition and you should protect your skin with suitable gloves or barrier cream. Once you have all the coating removed, oil all the bare metal surfaces lightly. A recommended oil is Rock Oil HLP32 Hydraulic Oil (not motor oil!) and a suitable grease for bearings and suchlike is Molyslip HSB grease.

Once the lathe is clean, you may need to fit some parts such as the tailstock and apron handwheels (Fig. 6.1). These are kept in place by either one or a combination of grubscrews that engage a flat on the shaft and an M8 nut. Avoid overtightening the nuts as this may cause the handwheels to bind.

## POWER TEST

Even if you plan to mount the lathe rigidly, it is a good idea to check the basic functions at this stage, but take precautions to ensure the lathe is mounted safely and securely so if it vibrates or shakes it will not fall or cause damage. Make sure any accessories, such as the chuck, are fitted securely and rotate the spindle by hand to make sure there are no mechanical clashes.

Make a visual inspection of the power lead and plugs for damage or bare wires. If all is well, then you can proceed through the initial starting procedure as given in your manual. This varies somewhat between models but is likely to be something like:

*Fig. 6.1 The handwheels are removed to reduce the risk of damage in transit.*

*Fig. 6.2 Lift this lever up to ensure power feed is disconnected and allow free movement of the saddle.*

*Fig. 6.3 Keep the tumbler reverse lever in neutral except when using power feed.*

Over about five minutes build up the spindle speed gradually to maximum and then run it for two or three minutes at full speed.

Stop the lathe using the emergency stop button.

Switch off the power and check everything is still safe and secure.

If the lathe has high/low gear, select 'high' and repeat this procedure.

Following this procedure will gently run in the gears and help maximize the life of the spindle bearings.

## MOUNTING THE LATHE

Before you embark on setting up your lathe, you should decide if it will be semi-permanently fixed in position. If so, it may be worth carrying out some of the setting up while you can still easily access the back of the machine but ideally the lathe should be adjusted when fixed or placed in its normal working position.

As supplied, the majority of mini-lathes have a swarf/drip tray fixed to the bottom of the bed by screws that also hold two fairly thick steel bars to the bottom of the machine. At the ends of these bars four rubber feet are fitted using M6 screws. The bars increase the 'footprint' of the lathe and make it more stable. It is possible to mount the lathe securely to a workbench either with long screws into the foot-mounting holes (with or without the feet in place) or, with the bars removed, directly into the bed.

Endless advice on mounting a lathe securely and ensuring the accurate alignment of the lathe bed has been given over the years. With larger lathes, it is usual to mount them to a very rigid metal bench and adjust the mountings carefully to ensure the lathe turns, as nearly as possible, parallel along its length.

In contrast, with small 'benchtop' lathes, it is not unusual for them to be used loose on the bench or simply fixed to a relatively light board. In this case, no strains are imposed

Ensure all pre-start precautions have been taken and, if the lathe has high/low gear, put it into 'low'. Close any guards as the lathe may not operate with them open.

Check the auto-feed is disengaged on the apron (Fig. 6.2) and the tumbler reverse lever is in neutral (Fig. 6.3). Move the saddle well away from the chuck.

Select forward rotation on the control panel and release the emergency stop switch.

Advance the speed control slowly until the machine starts and the spindle begins to revolve.

on the bed and, if it is accurate, then it will not be twisted.

Mini-lathes sit on the boundary between these two situations. Mounting the lathe on a large, heavy cabinet may seem over the top for such a modest machine, although at least one user has followed the path of casting a 75mm (3in) thick concrete slab on top of the bench and fixing the lathe to it.

If you want to go that far, or have a good solid, steel bench that won't warp or twist, you could benefit from removing the mounting feet and bars and securing the lathe bed rigidly, carefully aligning it. In this case, the rubber feet should be removed and replaced either with jacking screws or plain screws and adjusting shims. The classic account is in *The Amateur's Lathe* by L.H. Sparey (written at a time when *amateur* was still a compliment!) but, in brief, the basic technique is to hold a test bar in a three-jaw chuck and tighten the fixings gradually while monitoring test cuts to set the lathe so it turns as parallel as possible.

Many users simply use the lathe on top of a suitable bench or worktop, relying on the supplied rubber feet, and find this perfectly satisfactory. One reason why this can work is the very strong cross-braced design of the lathe bed, which is resistant to twisting. The problem with this arrangement is the a safety issue of leaving a lathe unsecured, as if the lathe is running fairly fast or with unbalanced work there is a possibility it could vibrate off the bench. Although it would be pretty negligent for such a situation to arise, it makes sense for the lathe to be secured in some way.

A simple solution is to use one of the relatively light but reasonably rigid mounting benches supplied for mini-lathes (Fig. 6.4). Another popular solution is to mount the lathe to a base, typically of plywood or 35mm (1½in) laminated worktop. This base can either be heavy or large enough to give the lathe extra stability, or can be clamped in place when the lathe is in use, but still allows it to be moved for access.

Fig. 6.4 This steel framed bench is supplied for use with mini-lathes.

Another approach to keeping the lathe constrained but not fixed rigidly is to recess four holes for the rubber feet in the bench top and fit long M6 screws through the bench and feet into the bottom of the lathe. These are then tightened enough to keep the lathe in place but not enough to compress the rubber feet or twist the bed.

A good arrangement was devised by Michael Cox, whose lathe is fixed to a 19mm chipboard benchtop. The rubber feet are not used. The lathe is mounted on two raising blocks made from 50 × 50 × 4mm hollow steel sections. The drip tray has been replaced by a much larger tray. At the head stock end, the raising block is bolted down tightly through the drip tray but at the tailstock end the raising block bolts are loose and serve only to locate the lathe. This way, the lathe is securely mounted but no twisting forces are applied to the bed.

In summary, if you have a very rigid base for your lathe, it is worth mounting it rigidly and adjusting it carefully for the best results. For most users with a less rigid wooden base, the best solution is to screw the lathe in position in a way that does not apply any forces to twist the bed. If you want the lathe to remain portable then consider some sort of simple restraint, such as wooden strips, to prevent the feet moving around the benchtop.

**Precautions and Preparations**

I don't apologize for starting with a reminder to switch off and unplug the machine before doing anything else! Quite clearly, these are not big lathes but even when inert they are still heavy and hence potentially dangerous objects. Before moving it around, have a think and decide if and when you may need some help. Ideally, for setting up move the lathe on to a small table where you can have easy access to all sides of the machine.

Working from the back of the machine, remove the screws holding on the splash guard (Fig. 6.5). This will create a lot more room and allow removal of the cross slide. Consider replacing the screws with 2BA studs and knurled brass nuts, or finger screws. Wind the top slide back until a pair of socket head screws are visible. When slackened these allow you to angle the top slide for taper turning. When removed you can lift the top slide off the cross slide. You now have good access to adjust the tailstock, saddle and cross slide.

*Fig. 6.5 Removing the splash guard will allow you better access.*

*Fig. 6.6 A bearing strip holds down the back of the saddle.*

*Fig. 6.7 The front bearing strip is hidden by the apron.*

## THE SADDLE

The saddle travels along the bed of the lathe, held in place by two strips bearing on surfaces under the edges of the bed (Fig. 6.6). These strips hold the saddle down on the bed and its 'inverted V', keeping it in alignment.

Any slack in the fit will result in side-to-side movement when engaging auto feed or changing direction with the hand feed. To set them properly you need to unscrew the 'apron' from the front of the slide and move it to the tailstock end of the bed. This is awkward to do as the clasp nuts will not allow the apron to be removed completely without removing the end bearing for the leadscrew. Moving the apron will reveal the bolts and grub screws for the front bearing strips. A similar set-up is rather easier to access at the back of the lathe. The grub screws adjust the fit, while the larger bolts actually hold the strips in position. There is some spring in the strips so there is some give and take between the two adjustments. Take care because if the grub screws are in too far, you will need to overtighten the bolts, bowing the strip and reducing its effectiveness.

Adjust the strips by loosening the bolts and then backing off the (lock nutted) grub screws (Fig. 6.7). Experiment with tweaking the bolts and grub screws until you can move the saddle back and forth by hand but with no movement if you try to wobble or twist the saddle on the bed. A fingertip on the junction of slide and bed is very sensitive to such angular movement. Another guide is to look for movement in the bead of oil along the junction of the sliding surfaces. You should be able to get the strips tightened evenly along their lengths but with no play and may well find the slide moving more freely than before you started. Do not overtighten the screws as the strips will bend, reducing the contact area and giving a less smooth movement.

### Lubrication

It is easy to forget to adjust or lubricate these strips but it is important that they, and all the other sliding and screwed movements of the lathe, are kept lubricated. You can use slideway oil but as this can be expensive many lathe owners just splash a bit of neat cutting oil on slides and leadscrews as they go along. Other owners use motor oil, although some people suggest the additives in this may cause problems and they use various plain oils. From this, you will probably deduce the exact nature of the oil you use isn't as critical as making sure you use *something* on a regular basis.

### THE HALF (CLASP) NUTS

Before you refit the apron, remove the screwcutting indicator from the right of the saddle, and take a good look at the half nut (Fig. 6.8). This assembly has its own gib strip, held down with screws and washers and adjusted by three grub screws in the apron (one hidden by the indicator). As supplied this assembly may be quite loose, with a good deal of play. You can remove this play by tightening the grub screws a little (Fig. 6.9).

You should also note the lock nutted stud that protrudes from the lower half nut. The function of this nut is to prevent the clasp nut from closing completely on the leadscrew. This may seem counterproductive, however a small piece of swarf on the leadscrew can affect how much it closes and effectively move the half nut position along enough to spoil a neat thread. This little stud ensures repeatability when cutting threads as the nuts always close by exactly the same amount. If you need to adjust it, back it out until the nuts will lock completely on to the leadscrew, wind the screw back in until the nuts just come loose on the leadscrew and then another quarter turn.

### APRON ALIGNMENT

If the apron is aligned poorly, closing the clasp nuts may noticeably deflect the leadscrew. If you tighten the apron fixing screws (Fig. 6.10) then back them off a little and close the clasp nuts, you should be able to retighten the fixing screws so the nuts can be opened and closed without causing any distortion of the leadscrew. This is best done with the saddle near the middle of the bed. Now re-attach the screwcutting indicator. You can leave it engaged all the time (there is very little load on it) but if you wish you can swing it out of engagement. The apron has a little side-to-side leeway in its position. I suggest fitting as far to the left as possible, as this will reduce the possibility of the cross slide handle fouling the apron handwheel.

Before we leave this area, it's worth contemplating the benefits of fitting a

*Fig. 6.8 Back of the apron showing the arrangement for the half nuts.*

*Fig. 6.9 The screwcutting dial needs to be removed to access the third half nut adjuster screw.*

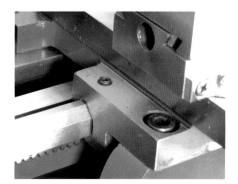

*Fig. 6.10 The apron fixing screws allow a certain amount of adjustment.*

guard of some kind over the leadscrew to help keep it free of swarf, as described in the upgrades chapter.

## CROSS SLIDE

Moving upwards, the next job is the cross slide. This has two adjustable components, a gib strip and a feed nut. On a new lathe excessive backlash (free play) in the slide screw is probably not a worn feed nut, it is more likely the nut is not properly secured. There are three screws accessible from the top of the slide itself, the smaller central grub screw sets the height of the nut, while the two outer screws hold it secure (Fig. 6.11). It is important the two outer screws are not just tensioned evenly but screwed in by the same amount so the nut is parallel to the leadscrew.

*Fig. 6.11 The cross slide feedscrew adjusting screws.*

Wind the slide right out until the nut disengages. Remove the central grub screw and gently tighten both the other screws. Now unscrew them both by exactly five turns. Then re-engage the feed screw – the two screws should lift slightly as the nut comes into line. If they don't lift, slacken them another turn. Screw the slide in almost as far as it will go – the nut should now be 'floating' but aligned perfectly. Screw in the grub screw until you can just feel resistance against the nut and now tighten the two other screws *by an equal number of turns* until the nut is held firmly. Do not overtighten or the screws could strip the

*Fig. 6.12 Three lock nutted grub screws adjust the cross slide gib.*

thread in the nut. Get this right and you will avoid excessive wear. If you find yourself experiencing gradual loosening of the nut, you might want to consider putting a small amount of thread-locking compound on the screws.

It is possible to angle the feed nut by adjusting the two screws once the neutral point is found, one up and the other down. I have seen this suggested as a way to eliminate any backlash in the nut. It quite possibly works in the short term but my concern would be that it could cause uneven and rapid wear. Bear in mind that backlash in the cross slide is not a huge problem as you normally take all cuts moving the slide in the same direction.

Three lock nuts and grub screws adjust the gib strip (Fig. 6.12), a long metal strip that forms one of the bearing surfaces for the dovetail joint between the base and body of the slide. These screws should all be tensioned evenly so there is no free play in the slide but one can turn the handle to move the slide in and out without excessive resistance. There is no special trick to this, just patience and care. It helps to hold the grub screw in place with an Allen key while tightening the lock nut. If you really can't get a smooth but rigid motion for the whole length of the slide's travel, remove the slide and inspect the gib strip. It may have a burr on one or more edges. This can be stoned

off with a small slipstone, a deburring tool or a fine file but be careful not to mark the sliding surface. A slipstone (small plastic-backed diamond coated slips work well) is also useful for many other jobs, including putting a keen edge on HSS toolbits.

## TOP SLIDE

Compared to the cross slide, the top slide is straightforward. There is no separate feed nut as the feed screw runs directly in the base, so you only have to check, lubricate and adjust the gib strip (Fig. 6.13). Like the cross slide, the top slide has three adjusters but, unlike it, it is possible for it to overhang the dovetails by a much greater proportion of its length. This means a certain amount of extra care and patience is needed to get the movement smooth at all points.

*Fig. 6.13 A similar arrangement adjusts the top slide gib.*

Fig. 6.14 Using a small engineer's square to check the topslide alignment.

**MOTOR DRIVE BELT**

It's worth removing the gearbox cover and checking the motor drive belt has adequate tension (Fig. 6.17). A sudden loss of power accompanied by a 'screeching' sound possibly means the motor has shifted on its mounts, loosening the toothed belt. A milder scraping sound may mean the toothed wheel has shifted on the shaft and the belt is rubbing on the guard. In both cases, switch off and adjust and realign or retension the belt.

Fig. 6.17 Both brushed and brushless versions use a toothed belt to drive the lathe.

The final job is to set the top slide square, much easier on this lathe than most. The top and cross slides are precision ground on all their faces so it is simply a matter of using a try square (Fig. 6.14). It's worth buying a small, say 75mm (3in), good quality engineer's square for this sort of job. The 'hack' carpenter's square lying around your workshop will probably be noticeably out for this sort of job.

Make a habit of always putting the top slide back square after any job that involves using it at an angle, especially if it has been set to a slight taper. Otherwise, it is easy not to notice that it is 'out', with obvious consequences.

**LEADSCREW BEARINGS**

The leadscrew is supported at each end by small plain bearings in blocks screwed to the lathe bed (Fig. 6.15). You will need to remove the gear cover to see the left-hand bearing block (Fig. 6.16). Some lathes have an oil sink or even a proper oil nipple on the blocks – mine has one of each – but some older versions just have plain bearing blocks with no oil ways. If your mini-lathe has no oil ways in these blocks, it is worth removing them and drilling a 1.5mm (¹⁄₁₆in) oil-way in the top of each one, carefully removing any burrs before replacing them. You may also find the leadscrew can move back and forth

along the bed somewhat. If this is the case, the mounting holes in the bearing blocks should be large enough to allow you to remove end play in the leadscrew but, if this is not quite possible, you can open up the mounting holes in the rear block slightly. Make sure the clasp nuts are engaged when repositioning the bearing blocks.

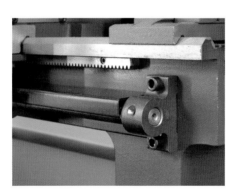

Fig. 6.15 Each leadscrew bearing block has an oiling point.

Fig. 6.16 The left hand block is inside the gearbox.

Adjustment on some lathes is done by moving the drive motor by winding one or more long 'grub' screws located in the front of the bed, between a pair of motor mounting screws, in and out (Fig. 6.18). Placed either side of the motor centre line, these have the effect of moving the motor up and down. This is something of a fiddly

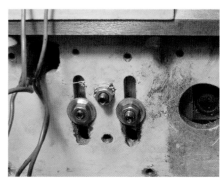

Fig. 6.18 Motor mounting and adjustment arrangements vary between versions, this is a CL300M.

job as you may need to loosen or tighten the mounting nuts between each adjustment of the grub screws.

On other versions of the mini-lathe, the motor is mounted on a pivot at the bottom of the motor space. Two adjustment screws are placed above and below the motor and are adjusted from the back of the machine with a spanner, after removing the motor cover. This is a considerably less fiddly arrangement.

The motor should be aligned horizontally and tension adjusted with one or the other of these up and down movements, not by angling the motor, which would cause the drive belt to rub. If you are exchanging motors, the toothed drive pulley may need to be swapped over – it has an internal key and is retained by a C-clip. A loose drive belt will result in slipping (accompanied by a startling noise!) under heavy loads. This is rarely a serious issue but if it happens too often the drive pulley and belt will wear badly and may need to be replaced. The larger driven toothed pulley is more lightly loaded, rarely slips and is unlikely to need replacement.

A complete loss of power without the dramatic sound effects could be the shearing of the moulded in key in the glass-filled nylon toothed wheel fitted on the end of the motor. This can happen if a machining error suddenly jams up the lathe under power – better than some more expensive part breaking! You can obtain replacement pulleys but as a get-you-going alternative file a groove inside the damaged wheel to match that on the motor shaft. You can then fit a small brass or steel key between wheel and shaft and have no more problems.

If you experience the sudden onset of rather rough running with a tendency for the motor to stall and blow a fuse it can be perplexing, especially if the job in hand is well inside the lathe's capacity. This can mean a worn out drive belt, which will can split and skip pulley teeth, stalling the cutter. Such a belt will soon gave way completely.

The answer is a replacement belt but these are cheap off the shelf items from the lathe suppliers. Removal of the old belt and fitting a new one simply requires removing the cover plate at the back of the headstock (you may need to remove any gears fitted to the lathe first) and re-tensioning the new belt.

## SPINDLE BEARINGS

It is important to be sure the spindle bearings in the lathe headstock are well adjusted as any looseness here will affect the accuracy and finish of your work and could cause chatter and other problems when taking heavier cuts or parting off. The basic test is the same whether you have deep groove ball bearings, angular contact bearings or roller bearings fitted. Fit the three-jaw chuck securely and run the lathe at a good speed for fifteen to twenty minutes to make sure it is well warmed up. Now fit a long steel bar of about 12-20mm (½in to ¾in) in the chuck. Using your fingers at the 'joint' between spindle and headstock (both front and rear), you should not be able to detect any sideways movement of the spindle when you pull the bar firmly back and forth. If you can detect movement then the bearings are too loose. Equally, when turning the spindle you should just be able to detect 'drag' from the bearings (don't confuse the resistance of the motor and drive train for tight bearings, disengage them if you are not sure). If the spindle turns really freely it is probably loose and if it has significant resistance it is too tight.

The bearings can be adjusted using two circular nuts at the back of the spindle (Fig. 6.19). These act on the bull wheel (the gear on the end of the spindle) and a spacer, which then presses on the centre race of the rear bearing. The outer nut is a lock nut and should be loosened slightly to allow the other nut to be turned to make a fine adjustment. This adjustment should be different depending on what type of

*Fig. 6.19 These two circular lock nuts adjust the spindle bearings.*

bearings you have (*see below*). After each adjustment, tighten the outer ring to lock.

### Bearing Lubrication

If you have deep groove ball bearings they probably have full seals and need no further lubrication. If you have angular contact or taper roller bearings then after extended use they may need regreasing. Clean out old grease with a clean tissue. Unless it is clearly contaminated or has gone hard, don't worry about getting it all off. If you intend to check them every few years then the best grease to use is a plain bearing grease or lithium grease. Apply enough to fill 20-25 per cent of the empty space in the bearing. If you want to 'fill and forget' use a moly grease but only aim to fill about 15 per cent of the empty space. These amounts may seem small but are in line with manufacturers' recommendations. Greater quantities of grease won't be squeezed out of the bearings at the modest speeds used by mini-lathes. Instead they will churn around and cause the bearings to overheat.

### Preload

Setting bearings can seem to be more of an art than a science. For critical applications such as CNC machines a careful procedure that involves monitoring the temperature of the bearings with an infrared thermometer is used. For our more modest machines we can take a simpler approach but be aware there is not necessarily one right answer. Bearings with less pre-load will last longer but those with greater preload will run more accurately. The main thing to avoid is the situation where the bearings are stiff or overheat during use.

Angular contact bearings or deep groove bearings should be tightened until all play disappears, then tightened a further quarter turn, then backed off very slightly to provide preload. If you have an early mini-lathe, then this should suffice. If you have a lathe with a more modern controller board with an automatic overload trip (look for an overload light on the control panel) bring the lathe slowly up to top speed. The motor controller should not trip even at top speed. You can add a little more preload and repeat the exercise until the motor just trips at top speed. Now back off the preload a little. Note that with the more powerful brushless motors, this procedure may result in slightly excessive preload, so watch out for the bearings overheating.

Taper roller bearings (Fig. 6.20) should be adjusted to the point where, at the usual operating temperature, there is no play.

Greatest bearing life is achieved with near zero or very slight preload. The design of taper rollers means they do not need greater preload to achieve accuracy.

Check the bearings do not run hot. Ideally they should just be warm to the touch after extended running under load. If they do run hot then there is either too much preload or, if they are open bearings, you may have put too much grease in them.

## THE TAILSTOCK

Offsetting the tailstock of a lathe makes it possible to turn modest tapers but, by the same token, if the tailstock is out of line work intended to be cylindrical will end up tapered! Accurate setting of the tailstock is also essential for good results when drilling, reaming or tapping with the tool held in the tailstock chuck. For good results you need to be sure the tailstock is aligned with the headstock and the barrel moves parallel with the lathe bed.

The tailstock is held in place by either a long lever at the back or a large bolt through its base. With the tailstock located securely, wind the barrel right out and try to wiggle it. There may be a fair amount of movement. Tightening up the locking lever on top of the tailstock should lock the barrel in position with good consistency.

*Fig. 6.21 Aligning centres in the headstock and tailstock by eye.*

*Fig. 6.22 Using a 'wiggler' to align the tailstock.*

Fig. 6.20 The inner race of a taper roller bearing, fitted to the lathe spindle but not yet lubricated.

If you just need a 'quick and dirty align-ment' you can align centres fitted in the head and tailstock by eye. If you are short-sighted or have a good hand lens or loupe, then this is a practical approach.

Wind the saddle up close to the head-stock. With a 3MT centre in the headstock and a 2MT centre in the tailstock their points should meet perfectly when the tailstock is slid up the bed (Fig. 6.21). If you have no 3MT centre, chuck an inch and a half piece of round brass or mild steel in the three-jaw chuck and turn a 60-degree point on the end. Once you have produced a point, don't take it out of the chuck as it will lose its accu-racy. Another alternative is to use a wiggler needle (Fig. 6.22) or a sticky pin set to run true but I find it easier to match two similar points against each other.

A better way of testing tailstock align-ment is using a thick bar with an accurate hole bored in it set between two centres (Fig. 6.23). Sighting across the length of bar to align it to the edge of the top slide will give a good result. The hole needs to be no more than about half the bar thickness in diameter otherwise the points of the two centres will clash.

Don't be surprised if the alignment is rather less than perfect, particularly when tried with the barrel locked in both the fully retracted and fully extended positions. You

Fig. 6.24 The two adjustment screws for the tailstock.

will probably find some judicious adjust-ment of the tailstock is in order. Note the vertical alignment should be spot on as this can only be adjusted by regrinding the head or tailstock! On the other hand, you may find the side to side adjustment to be well out as the tailstock is constructed in two parts to allow a deliberate offset for taper turning.

Two screws hold the two tailstock com-ponents together – a slotted grub screw at the rear and a cap head setscrew in the base (Fig. 6.24). Remove the main bolt that holds the tailstock captive and take it off the bed. Loosen both the adjustment screws and retighten so they barely grip the tailstock. You can now slide it from side to side and you will find there is the potential to twist it slightly as well.

If you have no dial test indicator (DTI), then setting up is a matter of twiddling until

the two centres are aligned properly with the tailstock both in and out.

If you do have a DTI, lock the tailstock barrel in the extended position (retracted by a turn or so – if wound right to the end it may twist slightly). Set the tip of the DTI on the side of the barrel and slide the tailstock back and forth by hand. You should find you can get the tips of the two centres lined up and the barrel parallel to less than 0.02mm (0.001in) along its length (Fig. 6.25). Tighten the two screws gently in stages, checking alignment as you go. Any error that creeps in can be corrected with a gentle tap from wooden mallet or the base of the handle of an ordinary hammer.

Fig. 6.25 Using a DTI to ensure the tailstock is not twisted to one side.

The tailstock barrel itself is not adjust-able but there is a small setscrew under-neath that acts as a key to stop it rotating or winding right out of the tailstock. Make sure it is properly in place (ensure it doesn't push the barrel upwards) and tighten its lock nut to avoid problems when drilling from the tailstock. The lever clamp that locks the barrel position is of the symmetri-cal split-clamp type. This is much better than the simpler cotter-pin arrangement as it does not lift the barrel at all, it just pushes it to one side and helps ensure that, even with some play, the barrel retains vertical accuracy.

If you want to achieve the very best results, you can turn a test bar between centres with a raised collar at each end. If

Fig. 6.23 Testing alignment with an accurate cross hole.

*Fig. 6.26 For the very best results, make a test bar and use it to align the tailstock.*

one collar is 'skimmed' and the bar reversed the other collar can be skimmed at the same setting. Both collars should now measure the same diameter. With this bar between centres you can use a dial test indicator in the toolpost to measure the location of the collars, once the DTI gives the same reading on each collar the tailstock is set correctly. Apply a little further 'fine adjustment' until they each give the same reading. In this way,

you should be able to set the tailstock so the lathe will turn parallel to 0.01mm (0.0005in) in 100mm (4in) or better. Keep the bar safe for future use.

**Final Tests**

First check all the various movements are smooth and can be accomplished without excessive force or any tight spots. The

spindle should run smoothly and quietly at all speeds without any sign of overheating.

Refer to the section on basic turning if you don't have previous experience of using a lathe. It should be possible to turn various test pieces and achieve reasonable rates of metal removal without 'chatter' or excessive noise and, at the other extreme, to take fine cuts with a sharp tool and achieve a good finish. Assuming the spindle is well adjusted and you are using a good tool at centre height, chatter and poor finish are probably signs of poorly adjusted slides.

Parting off a slice of 25mm (1in) diameter mild steel is a reasonably demanding task that will help you decide if all the gib strips are set properly and the bearings well-adjusted.

Finally, to check the alignment of the tailstock, mount a length of brass or steel bar between centres. Take a light cut along the length of the bar. If the diameters of the two ends are no more than about 0.02mm (0.001in) different or you can't feel any difference when gauging each end with a pair of calipers, then the set-up is pretty good.

# 7  Work Holding

Once set up, the lathe is ready to use but before you can actually start turning something, you have to fit a workpiece in the machine. For a quick start, the easiest approach is to grip a short length of bar in the three-jaw chuck and jump forwards to the chapter on basic turning. The lathe offers a far greater diversity of work holding methods and as you become more experienced you will find yourself using most, if not all, of them for different tasks. This chapter examines each approach and its strengths and weaknesses in detail.

## LATHE CHUCKS

As mentioned earlier, a lathe chuck is essentially a rotating vice. We will look in detail at the different types and their uses but the typical construction is a solid body, typically of steel or cast iron, with slots in which the gripping jaws can move. Except for small 'lever scroll' chucks, a T-handled chuck key is used for adjustment. On mini-lathes, the chucks are fitted to a backplate by M6 studs that pass through a flange on the end of the spindle. The studs should be nutted up firmly. This type of fitting has the advantage that the chuck is held secure whether running in forward or reverse, unlike lathes that have screw-on chucks.

The chuck is kept centred accurately by a small raised register on the flange that sits snugly in a recess on the back of the chuck (Fig 7.1). It is important the joining faces are kept scrupulously clean when changing chucks to ensure trapped swarf does not disturb the alignment. Changing chucks

*Fig. 7.1 An accurate recess in the back of this chuck ensures accurate alignment.*

*Fig. 7.2 The fiddliest tasks on a mini-lathe are removing and replacing the chuck fixing nuts.*

may be a fiddle at first – especially starting the nuts in the small gap between flange and headstock (Fig. 7.2). Once you have the 'knack', however, it is literally just the work of a minute or so to change them.

## THREE-JAW SELF-CENTRING CHUCK

An 80mm diameter self-centring chuck is standard equipment with mini-lathes (Fig. 7.3). It has three stepped jaws that move in and out together by virtue of a spiral or 'scroll' operated by socketed bevel gears on the outside of the chuck. A supplied 'chuck key' fits in the square sockets. You should find you have two sets of jaws described as 'inside' or 'outside', each of which will bear one or two numbers – one, two or three – and sometimes a serial number that matches one stamped on the chuck body (Fig. 7.4). You may also find one of the slots in the chuck body is numbered one but, if not, it is a good idea to remove the jaws carefully and mark the slot for jaw one using a centre punch. Note, you can't fit the jaws 'inside out' and this is why two sets are provided.

It is important to insert the jaws in the right order – if they are not, you will never get them to line up properly. If they are in

*Fig. 7.3 A standard self-centring three-jaw chuck.*

Fig. 7.4 Inside and outside jaws compared, showing the jaw and serial numbers.

Fig. 7.6 Using the inside step of the outside jaws can make it hard to access the work.

the right order, it is still possible for them to be misaligned. The easiest way to correct this is to wind the jaws outwards while pressing them gently inwards. Any jaws that are too far out from the centre will 'click in' as they pass the end of the scroll. Now, keeping up the pressure, reverse the scroll and wind them back in – properly aligned.

It is unusual that a standard mini-lathe chuck will have one of the sockets marked but if you buy a replacement or larger three-jaw you may find it has such a mark (often a '0'). This socket will be the one that has been found to give the most accurate results, so always use it when tightening the chuck.

The 'inside' jaws have their longest step near the centre of the chuck. They are called inside jaws because you normally grip

Fig. 7.5 Using inside jaws to grip a large disc by its bore.

things 'inside' them but you can poke them into a ring or bore and hold something by opening them out (Fig. 7.5). Nine times out of ten you will use them to hold relatively small, round work on its outside surface. You can also use them to hold a hexagonal bar or even rectangular objects, with one jaw on one side and two on the opposite side.

The 'outside jaws' are stepped inside and can be used to hold larger items – although if held on the inner step, the outer step can limit your ability to get a tool to the work (Fig. 7.6). The outside jaws can also be used to hold work such as flywheels on the inside of the rim.

Anything fitted in the chuck can be 'snugged' up against the face of the chuck or the steps in the jaws by tapping gently with a plastic or copper-faced hammer before the chuck is tightened fully. If you do this with care to something faced on one side, then reversed and faced on the other, the two sides will end up parallel enough for most purposes.

Although a chuck is described as self-centring, you cannot expect any plain three-jaw chuck to be perfectly concentric. Despite being inexpensive, the standard chucks supplied with mini-lathes are usually relatively good and if you clamp a length of 19mm (¾in) bar in the jaws you will probably find it runs true to within a few thou,

say 0.07mm. More expensive aftermarket chucks can give better results but even the most pricey three-jaw chucks rely on a micro-adjustable backplate that has to be tweaked for any particular diameter.

In practice, the three-jaw chuck is about convenience, not concentricity, and when you want to have multiple diameters in exact concentricity they should all be turned at one setting – that is without removing and replacing the work between cuts.

If you need to set an exiting circular surface perfectly concentrically, you should use the four-jaw chuck and a DTI as described later.

One thing that is rarely explained is how much force to use on the chuck key when tightening a chuck (Fig. 7.7). The answer is

Fig. 7.7 The length of the arms on a chuck key is matched to the force needed to tighten the chuck.

simple – the key is proportioned so that, if tightening it with one hand, a typical user is unlikely to overstrain it. So use one hand and steady pressure. You should avoid using both hands on the chuck key, jerking the key to 'nip it up' or using tubes or similar to extend the handles. Over tightening the chuck will damage the scroll and result in a gradual loss of accuracy and smooth operation.

Always make sure work is firm and secure in the chuck and bear in mind the forces involved in turning are surprisingly high, perhaps of the order of 30–40kg (60–80lb). Take care when using the chuck near its maximum capacity. Make sure all three jaws are engaged properly with the scroll and be aware if the jaws are only engaged with one or two turns of the scroll it is much easier to overstrain the chuck.

## FOUR-JAW INDEPENDENT CHUCK

You may be able to get a four-jaw chuck (Fig. 7.8) in a deal with your machine but if you do not, you will probably decide you need one fairly quickly as it has the capability of holding a much wider range of sizes and shapes of work. It is also able to hold work with greater concentricity than a three-jaw chuck.

The flexibility of the four-jaw comes from each reversible jaw having a separate adjusting screw so not just square, but even irregularly shaped, objects can be held. For objects longer in one dimension than another, you can reverse one or more jaws to get more reach. The separate screws mean the four-jaw can grip with rather more force than a three-jaw. As their thread finishes closer to the outer edge of the chuck than the scroll of a three-jaw, they usually have greater capacity as well.

Centring round work in a four-jaw chuck takes patience at first but with practice becomes second nature. Start by gripping the work more or less centrally by eye. You now need some means of determining how

Fig. 7.8 The obvious use of a four-jaw chuck is to hold square or rectangular objects.

Fig. 7.9 With careful adjustment, a four-jaw chuck can be used to set round work to run perfectly concentrically.

well it is centred. The ideal is a dial test indicator but for non-critical purposes the point of a surface gauge will do. Use the DTI to identify the highest point on the surface that needs to be made concentric with the lathe mandrel (Fig. 7.9). Loosen the jaw furthest from this point slightly, then tweak up the jaw nearest to the high point. Turn the work and see where the new high point is. Naturally, the amount to adjust the jaws will become less and less as you approach concentricity. Once the error is small enough you can usually just nip up the jaw at the high point without loosening the far jaw but take care not to overstrain the screws.

Another use of the four-jaw is for offsetting work for creating off centre holes or bosses (Fig. 7.10). Another example is when you need to make offset holes such as in a steam engine valve eccentric. This is achieved by turning the outside diameter, then setting the work in the four-jaw so the difference between the high and low points is exactly the required valve travel.

So, the four-jaw can do anything the three-jaw can do, and more. So why is a three-jaw always the chuck supplied with a new lathe? The answer is one word – convenience. For most purposes you need reasonable concentricity and a decent grip,

Fig. 7.10 A four-jaw chuck also allows work to be set eccentrically.

Fig. 7.11 A 4in chuck fitted to a mini-lathe using a backplate.

Although it is possible to purchase mini-lathes with a suitable spindle for fitting directly a 100mm chuck there are disadvantages. These include less availability of other accessories such as collet chucks, problems retro-fitting smaller chucks and, importantly, significant issues with using a faceplate. Fortunately, it is easy to fit a larger chuck using an intermediate backplate (Fig. 7.12) and enjoy the best of both worlds. Guidance on fitting a larger chuck is given in a later chapter.

Fig. 7.12 A ready-machined chuck backplate.

## CLEANING CHUCKS

Every time you place a piece of work in the chuck make sure the jaws are clean. An old toothbrush is a handy aid and can be pushed into the central hole to clean the whole length of the jaws. Storing chucks face down, with the jaws open, encourages swarf to fall out rather than dropping into the scroll or screws. You will find swarf collects on the scroll, no matter how much care you take. It can be removed by removing the jaws and using the toothbrush in the slots to sweep it out while you rotate the scroll/ screws.

Sometimes the chuck will lose some of its accuracy or have 'tight spots' no matter how well you have cleaned it in this way. This could mean it's time to dismantle the chuck, clean all the parts in paraffin or a

and the three-jaw gives you those in a few seconds. Most people use a three-jaw for everyday tasks but are glad to have a four-jaw handy for when they need its flexibility.

## OTHER CHUCKS

Other types of chuck you may come across occasionally include the six- and four-jaw self-centring types. The six-jaw chuck is particularly good for holding a thin-walled tube – a standard three-jaw is as good, if not better, for holding a hexagon bar. The four-jaw self-centring chuck is idea for square bars and can be used to hold round work.

Less commonly, you might even find an eight- or two-jaw chuck but generally the three-jaw self-centring and four-jaw independent chucks will cope with most tasks.

## BIGGER CHUCKS

The one area in which you might find the standard chucks rather limiting is in their size, particularly the 80mm three-jaw chuck. Increasing to a 100mm (4in) chuck may not seem like a big increase but in practice this gives nearly a 50 per cent increase in the diameter of work that can be held in the inside jaws, a significant benefit (Fig. 7.11).

similar solvent, regrease and reassemble it. The process is reasonably straightforward. With a three-jaw, you start by unscrewing the plate sunk into the back of the chuck then you remove (and number or mark) each part in turn, taking great care to ensure each one goes back where it came from. Do not feel you need to do this regularly. I have only disassembled my chucks in this way at intervals of several years.

## SPLIT BUSHES AND MANDRELS

At times you may want to be absolutely sure work is held truly concentrically. Let's say you want easier repeatability than a four-jaw chuck but do not have any collets. The simple way of achieving this is a split bush, bored in situ to a good fit on the work or drilled and reamed if the bore is small. A 'top hat' shape is convenient, as it can be positively located against the chuck jaws (Fig. 7.13). If the slit is made opposite to jaw number one, you can have a sporting chance of locating it accurately again in the future.

Fig. 7.13 A simple split bush for holding slender round work accurately.

Most scrap can be used to make such a bush but brass is a good material as it is easy to work accurately and to a good finish while having a degree of 'springiness'.

For hollow work, a mandrel that fits

Fig. 7.14 A selection of mandrels for holding work with a central hole accurately.

inside the work is needed instead (Fig. 7.14). Turned in place, such a mandrel will be 100 per cent accurate. If you turn such mandrels from offcuts of hexagon material (marked for number one jaw) they can be reused for less critical applications.

The mandrel should be turned to a tight fit, relieved to give a slight taper at the outside end. This is the most accurate solution but the danger is always there that the work will skid and be scored on its bore. A threaded end for a nut and washer, or tapped for a screw and washer, can be used to hold most work secure. An alternative, ideal when you need to be able to turn the whole face of the work, is to thread the mandrel under size for a large screw (just use the tip of a taper tap), then split it with a neat saw cut. Once fitted inside the work it can be expanded with a suitable screw.

## WORKING WITHOUT A CHUCK

In the good old days a new lathe typically arrived without either a motor or a chuck. Most turning would have been done either between centres or with the work fixed to a large disk, called a faceplate.

## THE FACEPLATE

Mini-lathes are not typically supplied with a faceplate but if you decide to tackle larger or awkward jobs, such as machining irregularly shaped castings, then a faceplate will be

essential (Fig. 7.15). The faceplate is simply a large cast iron disc, fitted in the same way as a chuck, to which work can be screwed securely or clamped. Standard mini-lathe faceplates have radial slots for use with T-nuts (Fig. 7.16). It is possible to make your own faceplate (some people have used weightlifting weights as the raw material) and then you have the choice of slots, T-slots or even a pattern of drilled and tapped holes and arranged as you see fit.

Fig. 7.15 The faceplate can allow you to tackle jobs that are far too large or awkward to hold in a chuck.

The two issues with using the faceplate successfully are security and balance. You need to remember cutting forces in a lathe can be quite high, so simply clamping something down might not always be sufficient. For greater security, consider if you need to attach further clamps or stops to ensure the work cannot rotate or slip under cutting forces. Although the larger

Fig. 7.16 A set of clamps, screws and nuts to suit a mini-lathe faceplate.

diameters turned on the faceplate usually mean running the lathe slowly, if the work is badly out of balance you are likely to experience significant vibration. When the work is balanced and with the lathe out of gear, you should be able to spin the faceplate and the work will come to rest at a random orientation. The easiest way to achieve balance is simply by bolting suitably sized lumps of metal to the light side of the faceplate.

In order to fit a faceplate you will have to remove the chuck guard. Combined with the fact that faceplate work will almost certainly be surrounded by protruding clamps and screws, it is essential to take extra care to keep things secure and hands and clothing well clear of the rotating work. This is a situation in which having a simple movable clear plastic guard screen, ideally on a magnetic base, is very useful.

A typical use of the faceplate is to turn a flywheel that is too large to hold in a chuck. Clamped carefully (it is easy to snap or distort the spokes of a flywheel) so it is packed clear of the faceplate itself, the flywheel is normally set so the inner rim runs concentrically. It is then possible to machine the hub and bore of the flywheel as well as one face and the rim, all at the same setting. This helps make sure the flywheel won't wobble when fitted. The flywheel is flipped for machining of the other face but no further work is done on the bore or rim.

## TURNING BETWEEN CENTRES

The very oldest lathes were simply a frame with two opposed, stationary points (centres) between which the work was mounted and turned by means of a cord worked by a bow or treadle. Both the green woodworker's pole lathe and the delicate watchmaker's 'turns' are examples of such 'dead centre' lathes and, although primitive, they have the curious property of inherently generating truly circular work. Today, it sometimes seems the technique of 'turning between centres' is falling into disuse, yet it offers other advantages, not least that work can be removed and replaced in the lathe with 100 per cent repeatability.

On metalworking lathes, centres are mounted in the lathe headstock (live centre) and tailstock (dead centre) and adjusted to

support the work firmly, but not tightly, using conical centres holes drilled in each end (Fig. 7.17). The 'dead centre' should be well lubricated and care taken not to push it too tightly into the work with the tailstock otherwise it will overheat, bind and rapidly ruin both itself and the centre hole in the work. Alternatively, a rotating centre (also confusingly called a live centre by some) can be used in the tailstock. Such a centre will have thrust and radial bearings and let considerable force be used to support the work more firmly, allowing heavier cuts to be taken.

The holes in the work are normally drilled with the work supported in a chuck, perhaps with the assistance of a fixed steady for long items, although in some circumstances you may need to use a pillar drill. If you do this, bear in mind centres drilled 'off the lathe' are unlikely to be perfectly aligned. A proper centre drill should always be used so the centre of the conical hole is relieved; this ensures the work seats cleanly and the centre hole also provides an oil reservoir for the dead centre.

To rotate the work between centres, a device known as a 'driving dog' is attached to the work and driven by a catchplate fitted to the spindle. The catchplate is like a small faceplate and would normally have either a slot or a protruding bar. The dogs have a hole and screw to clamp to the work and

Fig. 7.17 A small crankshaft held between centres. Missing from this shot are a driving dog and catchplate.

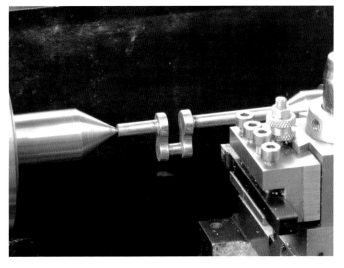

one of two types of 'tail' – straight to be used with a bar or bent to be used with a slotted catchplate.

Historically, lathes were typically supplied without a chuck of any kind but with a faceplate and a catchplate (Fig. 7.18). Curiously, no one appears to produce a catchplate for mini-lathes, although it is easy enough to make one to fit the spindle from a piece of steel of about 4in (100mm) diameter and ½in (13mm) thick. Alternatively, for larger work a stud screwed to the the faceplate can be used or for smaller items an 8mm bar with a short M6 screw thread on its end can be fitted in one of the spindle flange holes to serve as a driver. A 'bodge' that actually works well is to hold a short length of bar in a three- or four-jaw chuck and turn a 60 degree point on its end. This is then used as the live centre and the drive for a 'bent tail' dog can be taken from one of the chuck jaws.

*Fig. 7.18 The catchplate of a small lathe. For mini-lathes it is necessary to improvise or make your own.*

Some of the tasks well suited to work between centres include connecting rods and crankshafts – indeed any lengthy work that needs to be turned accurately and concentrically. Between centres this is achieved by turning one end and then reversing the work, taking care to use a thin metal shim or other protection so the lathe dog does not damage the freshly turned surface. The inherent accuracy of working between centres should ensure the overlap between the cuts made from each end are essentially

invisible. If you can 'see the join' it should be small enough to polish out with fine emery cloth.

Turning between centres may appear fiddly and even hazardous – you need to take care to ensure the lathe dog or catchplate arrangement can't catch tools, fingers or clothing – but do it successfully and you will start to feel like a 'real' turner.

## TYPES OF CENTRE

Centres can be used for turning between centres but also to support work held in a chuck or on a faceplate. Although they appear simple, there are many different types available.

### Fixed Centre

A fixed centre is really simple, just a 60 degree point on the end of a suitable taper (Fig. 7.19). Its disadvantage is it needs to be kept well lubricated and it should not be forced into the work – the task is to resist sideways forces not end to end ones. If you overdo it then the work may be damaged or you could even score the centre itself. Fixed centres are normally hardened or even have carbide inserts. Mini-lathe users should have an MT2 one for the tailstock and an MT3 one for the headstock, unless they also have a soft centre.

### Soft Centres

Nothing to do with confectionery, these are relatively soft, or at least unhardened, centres meant for use in the headstock, where they rotate with the work and therefore are not subject to significant wear. For a mini-lathe, you need an MT3 one. For critical jobs, you can angle the top-slide to 60 degrees and take a light skim off the centre while it is in position, ensuring it is perfectly concentric.

### Half Centre

Half centres are useful little beasts. Used in the tailstock, they are cut away to allow you to machine right up to the end of very small work, even taking facing cuts (Fig. 7.20). Clearly they cannot rotate so, like any fixed centre, they need to be well lubricated and not used too tightly. Sometimes it pays to use a rotating centre and then swap to the half centre just to finish the last bit.

### Cutting or 'Square' Centre

A square centre is an old alternative to a centre drill (Fig. 7.21). It is not used to support the work, instead it is used to open out a drilled hole into a conical shape that can be used with a traditional centre. They are fairly uncommon these days but if you

*Fig. 7.19 Headstock (MT3) and tailstock (MT2) centres compared.*

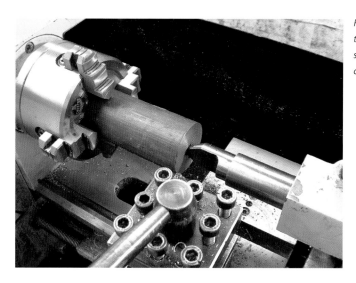

*Fig. 7.20 It can be possible to face right across work supported by a half-centre.*

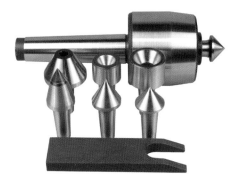

*Fig. 7.24 A rotating centre with a set of interchangeable 'noses'.*

*Fig. 7.21 Rarely encountered, but still with its uses, the square centre can tidy up a poor centre.*

They are available in many different levels of quality according to the type of bearings used, their accuracy and the level of side thrust they can cope with.

Various different specialist types of rotating centre are available.

**Reduced Centre**

With a similar purpose to a half centre, the reduced centre is a rotating centre with a less robust end cone that gives improved access to the work.

*Fig. 7.22 A rotating centre can provide more effective support than a fixed centre.*

can get one in good condition cheaply, do so. They are excellent for restoring damaged centre holes as they are much more robust than centre drills.

**Rotating Centre**

The easiest type of centre to use is the rotating type (Fig. 7.22). Just pop in the tailstock and advance into the work until it is supported adequately (Fig. 7.23). It needs no lubrication and can take more pressure than a fixed centre, although you should beware of using too much pressure as you could distort the work. A rotating centre is also useful for applying pressure to a large workpiece held in a chuck or on the faceplate for added security.

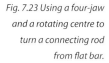

*Fig. 7.23 Using a four-jaw and a rotating centre to turn a connecting rod from flat bar.*

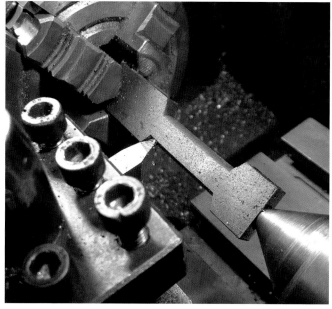

## Cone Centre

This is a rotating centre with a larger than usual end, perhaps as much as 50mm (2in) or more in diameter. It is used for supporting the end of tubular work.

## Hollow Centre

Occasionally you may need to support work that cannot be centred. One solution is a cone centre that can cup the end of the work. They are usually of the rotating type.

## Spherical Centre

The spherical centre has a hardened ball on the end. This can be used in a relatively deep centre to support work being turned to a taper between offset centres. It provides a better support than a conical centre in these circumstances but should still be well lubricated. Normally these are used in pairs, one in the tailstock, one in the headstock. An alternative is to use a large ball bearing supported in a hollow centre.

## Choosing a Centre

If you only have one tailstock centre, it's worth investing in a rotating centre – then you can forget worrying about lubricating a dead centre or worrying about how much pressure to apply. It's possible to obtain sets that contain a rotating centre together with a selection of different 'noses' for different types of work – nice to have but not essential. It's often possible to pick up different types of centre cheaply at boot sales or shows but make sure they are in good condition as a damaged one will just cause frustration.

## COLLET CHUCKS

A collet is a tubular work holding device, usually of metal, and with slits along its length that works by squeezing the work or the shank of a tool (Fig. 7.25). Collets are generally made to work at a single size or a small range of sizes at best so they are usually both accurate and repeatable. Although some types of collet are available in different accuracy grades, usually even the most basic type offers accuracy better than most three-jaw chucks and greater convenience than setting work to run true in a four-jaw chuck.

Fig. 7.25 A trio of ER25 collets.

Collet chucks are very useful when you want to hold round items accurately without the need to spend ages adjusting them for concentricity.

A bewildering array of collet types are available Each type has different strengths but there are three types you are most likely to encounter.

## MT3 Collets

These are very simple, single size, collets that fit the lathe taper. The flanged spindle nose means only drawbar versions can be used with mini-lathes. They are usually available only in a relatively limited range of sizes and their chief advantages are they offer very small overhangs and are very simple to use with the MT3 taper of the mini-lathe spindle.

## C5 Collets

C5 collets are a very popular series of collets intended for work holding and often used with milling fixtures. They require a holding chuck that can be operated by a drawbar, closing nut or, most usefully, be held in a key operated chuck. They are single size but are available in many sizes in 1mm or $\frac{1}{32}$in steps and with hexagon and square holes. Bear in mind a full set is very expensive. If you want to hold hexagon and square stock regularly as well as round material, then C5 may be the choice for you. The biggest problem is C5 collect chucks are quite big – typically 125mm (5in) diameter – and will need a backplate for fitting to a mini-lathe.

## ER Collets

There are many series of ER collet (Fig. 7.26), including ER11, ER16, ER25, ER32 and ER45 (defined by their outer diameter in millimetres). They have the advantage of each covering an 'extended range' (typically 1mm above 3mm nominal size). Used with a matching collet chuck, they were designed originally for tool holding but are ideal as work holding collets if you want to be able to hold both round materials and tools in virtually any size.

The ER25 and ER32 size collets have proven popular with many mini-lathe users as they are relatively inexpensive and can be 'shared' with a milling machine. Another advantage is that only twelve collets will cover every size in the range 3 to 16mm (about $\frac{1}{8}$in to $\frac{3}{8}$in). Imperial collets are also available and some users buy $\frac{1}{4}$in and $\frac{1}{2}$in collets rather than squeeze down 7mm and 13mm collets for these frequently used sizes. The collets are fitted using a special nut into which they 'click' and this makes removal very easy. Ball bearing nuts are available and these reduce the closing torque considerably.

ER25 and 32 collet chucks are available with a flanged fitting for direct attachment to mini-lathes (Fig. 7.27). These are rather smaller than C5 collet chucks and, occupying about the same amount of space as a normal chuck, they also allow stock to extend right through the chuck.

Alternatively, chucks with an MT3 taper

*Fig. 7.26 An ER25 collet chuck with an MT3 shank.*

*Fig. 7.27 An ER32 collet chuck that fits directly onto a mini-lathe spindle flange.*

can be readily sourced or it is possible to get started very cheaply with ER collets by buying one or two collets in useful sizes and making your own collet chucks using an MT3 blank arbour. It is common to buy a closing nut as these are very fiddly to make. Ball bearing closing nuts are available at very modest cost.

## COLLET STYLES TO AVOID

There are a few types of collet chuck that really don't suit lathe use because they are made primarily for holding cutters rather than workpieces.

*Fig. 7.28 An Osborn Titanic II chuck. This takes screwed end milling cutters and is not suitable for holding stock.*

### Collets for Screwed End Mills

These are special collets for end mills with a screwed shank, available in a few different styles and in a limited range of diameters to suit milling cutters. The most common are the Clarkson and Osborn Titanic designs and their overseas 'clones' (Fig. 7.28). While they can be used to hold milling cutters in the lathe, they are not suitable for holding stock and have been widely replaced for tool holding by ER collets in industry.

### Proprietary Expanding Collets

There are many systems of collet that bear more than a passing resemblance to ER collet systems. While these may well be an economic solution to tool holding in a milling machine, they rarely have the range of ER collets and are often only available in a more limited range of sizes. While they can be an economical solution to holding end mills, it is worth getting ER collets if you want to use them for work holding.

# 8    *Lathe Tools*

If you imagine a short length of bar held in a lathe chuck, there are some obvious ways to remove metal from the bar:

- Cut along the outside of the bar. This is normal turning (Fig. 8.1)
- Cut across the front end of the bar to create a flat surface. This is known as facing
- Cutting a hole into end of the bar. This is called boring
- Cutting a groove into the bar, which done deeply enough will separate the end from the rest of the bar. This is parting off or just parting.

A fifth simple task is to angle any of the corners produced where two of the above cuts meet each other. This is called chamfering.

Naturally, a lathe is capable of many more operations than this but these five basic operations will probably account for the majority of work you do. Each operation calls for its own special tools and actions, so we will look at them in detail. First, some general points about tools.

## HOW LATHE TOOLS CUT

Only the shallowest of cuts in metals can be made with a slicing action, like that of a wood plane. Most of the time lathes cut by forcing the edge of a tool beneath the surface of the work. The surface layer shears off as a chip, which slides across the surface of the tool. The energy expended in cutting is mostly expended as heat at the tool tip, which softens the metal and eases the cut, or as the chip rubs across the top of the tool, which just heats it up. In industry, the heat may be so great the swarf glows red- or even yellow-hot and even a mini-lathe worked hard is capable of making 'blue' chips.

The design of lathe tools seeks a balance between maximizing metal removal and achieving a good finish. Naturally, different materials and cutting operations require different shapes of tool. The various rakes and angles of a cutting tool serve two purposes. The face and end of the tool have relief (are angled away from the work) to ensure they do not rub. The top of the tool is also angled (top rake) to enable the creation of the chip. For soft material such as aluminium, the cutting edge can be sharply angled as it does not have to be very strong. For tougher materials, including steel and cast iron, a blunter angle is needed. For materials such as brass, which breaks naturally into small chips, a so called 'negative rake' tool, or at least a flat topped ('zero rake') one, can be used. The less top rake, the more shearing rather than slicing will dominate the cutting action.

Lathework demands all sorts of cuts, from heavy 'roughing cuts' to fine 'finishing cuts', facing, parting off and contouring, and all in different sorts of materials at different speeds and diameters. Clearly just

*Fig. 8.1 Turning along the length of the bar.*

one type of tool is not going to serve for all these roles but fortunately there are a few standard tool types that will deal with most situations. It's also worth remembering the quality of the tool is more important than having all the angles spot on, so concentrate on getting a selection of good quality tools rather than trying to have a different tool for every last material you may find in the workshop.

## FITTING TOOLS

Tools are simply fitted in any of the four stations in the toolpost by clamping down on them with two or three of the fitting screws as appropriate (Fig. 8.2). The screws should be tightened firmly but not overtightened. A standard 5mm Allen key is about 100mm (4in) long and you should be able to adequately secure any tool in the toolpost with just two screws by turning such a key with one hand.

Although it is possible to fit four tools in the toolpost at once, you will probably rarely have more than two tools fitted at any one time – more than this and the profusion of sharp edges pointing back at you becomes awkward, if not something of a hazard.

Check the four-way toolpost is properly aligned – it has four notches underneath that engage with a detent on the top slide.

Loosen the clamp lever a little and twist the toolpost anti-clockwise to select the tool you need, then turn it back a little against the stop and tighten up the clamp. This allows you to use one tool, rotate to another and then go back to the original tool but you should realize the arrangement is not perfectly repeatable.

## SETTING TOOLS AT CENTRE HEIGHT

When you buy tools or make your own to the normal patterns, they are designed to work at their best, as is the lathe itself, when the cutting edge is fed in horizontally across or along the diameter of the work. To do this, the cutting edge just needs to be set at the lathe's centre height. It is not difficult to do this. Most mini-lathes are designed so when an 8mm or ⁵⁄₁₆in tool bit is held in the four-way toolpost, its top surface will be just below centre height. Adjustment is just a matter of adding one or more thin metal spacers (shims) below the tool to raise it to the correct height. An ideal material for shims is to cut 1 × 4cm (⅜ × 1½in) strips from soft drink cans. A dead centre fitted in the lathe mandrel will provide a point exactly at centre height, so just shim up each tool you have until its cutting edge is aligned with the point of the centre. As drink can shim is virtually free you can make a set for each

tool and keep them together with rubber bands.

The smaller 6.35mm (¼in) tools often supplied for mini-lathes come with a holder that, when used with the four-way toolpost, will put the cutting edge on centre height but check to be sure.

Despite much you may hear, 'exactly on centre height' is a counsel of perfection and the closest you can get by adding or subtracting one shim of this kind is perfectly adequate for all normal turning.

A good test of a tool being set correctly is to take a light cut across the face of a workpiece. A correctly set tool will leave no centre pip, although it is better for it to be slightly low than high and a minute 'witness' is acceptable (Fig. 8.3). Obviously this works only for tools that can take a facing cut but in practice most tool shapes are capable of a tiny shaving cut.

Fig. 8.3 Facing across the end of a bar.

One thing I have never seen mentioned is how to set tools with sloping cutting edges – obviously only one part of the edge can be at centre height! Set the highest point that will be cutting to centre height to ensure the tool does not rub.

## TYPES OF TOOLS AND THEIR USES

Another way to classify turning operations is into 'roughing' or finishing, the difference being that roughing concentrates on the rapid removal of material while finishing

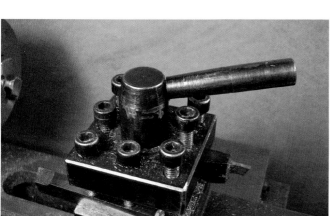

Fig. 8.2 A right-hand knife tool and a parting tool in the toolpost.

tools aim to get a part dead to size with a good surface finish.

Roughing tools are often more robust and may have obtusely angled ends to produce wider, thinner chips. Finishing tools will have relatively sharp ends, although the cutting edge is usually curved or has a small flat on it to help ensure a smooth finish.

Owing to the relatively modest size of mini-lathes, roughing cuts are rarely really heavy and many users will use the same tool for roughing and finishing. The wise will always do a quick check to ensure the tool is still sharp before making the last few finishing cuts. Nothing is worse than making a last cut perfectly to size and getting a finish like a ploughed field from a chipped tool!

Let's take a detailed look at some of the types of tool used with mini-lathes.

## READY GROUND HSS TOOLS

Most suppliers of mini-lathes also sell sets of HSS lathe tools. I would recommend you get one of these for a number of reasons. Importantly, HSS cuts well at low speeds and feeds and can give good results in the hands of a beginner who would prefer to 'take it easy' while they get used to their new machine. Secondly, you will soon want to start grinding your own tools. Being able to compare the angles of a set of pre-ground tools makes it easier to understand the ideas of rake and clearance. Finally, these sets usually contain sufficient tool shapes for you to experiment with turning, facing, boring and even screwcutting without great expense.

One set uses 6.35mm (¼in) shank tools, some of which are double ended, that come with a special holder that sets them at centre height with reasonable accuracy without the use of shims (Fig. 8.4). It may well be worth getting one of these sets just for the holder as it is easier to grind your own tools from smaller section HSS.

Fig. 8.4 *This holder is intended to place ¼in (6.3mm) square tools at mini-lathe centre height.*

Fig. 8.6 *Round and square HSS toolbit blanks.*

## GRINDING YOUR OWN HSS TOOLS

With a suitable grinder equipped with a stable rest it is possible to grind your own HSS tools. Figure 8.5 shows a selection of HSS bits. Bit A is a thin parting tool for cutting off small stock or making narrow grooves. B is a standard solid parting tool, C is a sharp pointed knife tool while D is similar but with a flat on the end for an improved surface finish. Bit E has a rounded end for creating a fillet in a corner and F is a screw-cutting tool. All but bit B were ground using no more than a standard bench grinder with a decent rest.

HSS is available as 'blanks' in a large range of sizes and shapes – round, square and thin rectangular for parting tools (Fig. 8.6). The best way to cut HSS blanks to length is with a thin abrasive cut-off wheel in a Dremel or similar rotary tool. It is not necessary to cut the whole way through the blank, just make a deep score line all the way round. Put the blank in a vice with the score just above the jaws, cover it with a heavy cloth and clout the end with a hammer. The cloth

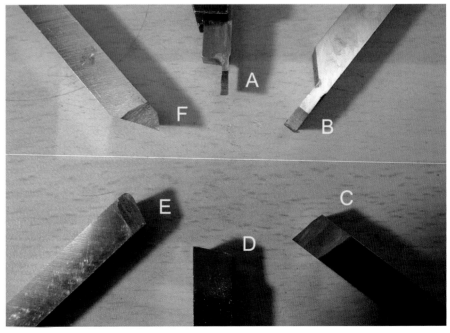

Fig. 8.5 *A selection of HSS bits. See text for details.*

is essential to catch the broken piece and any flying chips. The easy way to start grinding your own HSS tools is to copy the angles and shapes of existing tools but it is worth looking at the knife tool in detail.

## THE KNIFE TOOL

The knife tool is one that will serve for the great majority of turning and facing operations (Fig. 8.7). It is a fairly simple shape that essentially has a straight cutting edge that slopes away from the work below the cutting edge as well as on the top and at the front (Fig. 8.8). The relief at front and below the edge is to ensure the tool doesn't rub and that on the top (top rake) reduces the wedge angle where the tool is forced into the work. The smaller the wedge angle, the more the action of the tool is by cutting rather than shearing, reducing the force required. For certain metals, such as

brass or cast iron that produce dust like or small chips, the top rake can be zero – that is a flat topped tool. For steels and other metals that produce more or less continuous swarf then 10 degrees or more of top rake is useful. For very soft metals such as aluminium, even more top rake can be used (Fig. 8.9).

It is beneficial to put a small radius in the tip of the tool. This makes it less brittle and helps improve surface finish – as does a short flat ground or stoned on the end just behind the cutting tip. A larger radius tip can be used to leave a fillet when turning into a corner.

It is fairly simple to grind a knife tool 'offhand' from a piece of 8mm (⁵⁄₁₆in) tool steel, although beginners can benefit from using a card template to help set the angles. A standard bench grinder is fine for sharpening lathe tools. For HSS, the medium and coarse grit wheels supplied

*Fig. 8.9 This tool for use with aluminium alloy and plastic has a very steep top rake.*

with most grinders will be ideal. Always follow the safety instructions with a grinder, in particular never use a wheel that is damaged (an intact wheel will 'ring' if tapped gently with a screwdriver), unbalanced or rated below the speed of the grinder. Never use a second-hand wheel or one without its rating label fitted. Wear eye protection and always let the wheel come up to speed when standing to one side of it. A grinding wheel bursting can be very unpleasant and grinders are one of the most common causes of machining accidents in industry.

Note that 'offhand' doesn't mean you just hold the HSS in your hand and poke it into the grinding wheel! It just means the work is not clamped to the grinder. You should always use a grinding rest set close to the wheel to stop the work from being pulled in or jamming the wheel and ideally it should have a 'fence' to guide the tool at the correct angle. It pays to make simple card or plastic angle templates to help you angle the grinding rest correctly and to present the HSS at the correct angle. Don't rush the grinding and don't overheat the work. Don't dip the HSS in water to keep it cool – this can make it liable to crack or chip in use. HSS can quite happily be raised to red heat without losing its hardness, unlike carbon steel. Use a clamp to hold the toolbit if you find your fingers are overheating!

To make the knife tool, start with the grinding rest set so it creates an angle of about 100 degrees with the edge of the

*Fig. 8.7 A left-handed knife tool.*

*Fig. 8.8 The various angles on the tip of a knife tool.*

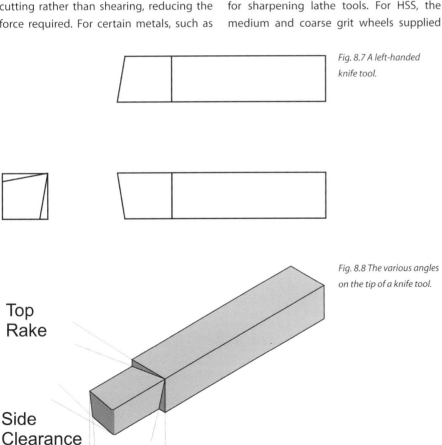

Top Rake

Side Clearance

Front Clearance

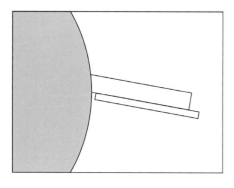

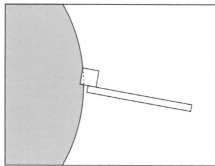

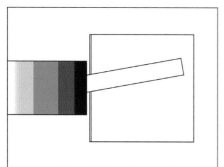

*Fig. 8.10 Shaping the end of the knife tool.*

*Fig. 8.11 Grinding the front clearance.*

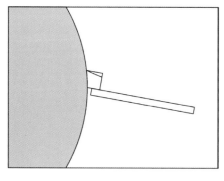

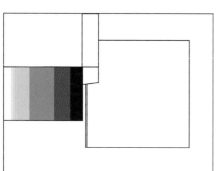

*Fig. 8.12 Grinding the top rake.*

sideways to the wheel and grind a clearance angle along about 8mm (⁵⁄₁₆in) at the tip (Fig. 8.11). Aim to make the relieved section just reach the angle along the top edge. Now turn the blank end for end and rotate it 90 degrees so you can grind the top rake. You are aiming to create a sharp corner by grinding until you just meet the previously ground face (Fig. 8.12). For a zero-rake tool for brass, omit this last step. For a steeply raked tool for aluminium, you can increase the angle of the rest by several degrees.

You now have the basic tool but the very tip will be sharply pointed and therefore weak. To strengthen it and improve the finish, you can grind or stone a flat on the tip, keeping the same clearance angle (Fig. 8.13.B). If you take it carefully, you can either put a small radius on the tip or more easily grind a few small facets to approximate a curve (Fig. 8.13.C). If you want a sharp tip, just dress the vertical corner with a slipstone or diamond slip but it may not stay sharp as long.

A relatively small radius, say 1mm (0.040in) is good for general use but you can use a bigger radius for making a nice fillet in shouldered corners (Figs 8.13.D, 8.14). Such fillets are useful as they reduce stress and increase the fatigue life of components.

wheel. If you place the HSS blank on the rest angled sideways at 10 degrees, this will allow you to gently shape the end of the tool (Fig. 8.10). Note that HSS blanks usually have angled ends, a helpful feature that reduces greatly the amount of metal you need to remove.

The next step is to turn the blank

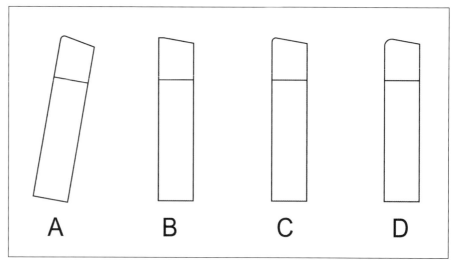

*Fig. 8.13 Various alternative shapes for the tip of the knife tool (see text).*

*Fig. 8.14 A large tip radius can be used to make filleted corners.*

## TANGENTIAL TOOLS

Tangential tools, or rather tangential toolholders, are designed to take square and/or round toolbits and present them to the work almost vertically. By making use of the cross-section of the toolbit and angling it correctly, a toolpoint with excellent geometry can be made simply by grinding the top of the tool at the correct rake angle. Some such toolholders come with a simple grinding jig for the ultimate in simplicity.

From much of what is said about tangential tooling, you might assume it is some remarkable new invention. In fact, tangential toolholders have been around for at least a century. Neither are they inherently better than other types of HSS tooling – it's quite possible to grind a conventional tool with exactly the same geometry – so why are they so popular? The answer is in how simple they are to set up and sharpen. When the tangential tool becomes blunt, just take a lick off the top and it's good to go.

The downside to tangential tools is the difficulty of making the toolholder, with the need to cut various compound angles to a good degree of accuracy, although a simplified design by Michael Cox was published in *Model Engineers' Workshop*. You can obtain ready-made tangential toolholders, such as the Diamond toolholder from Eccentric Engineering (Fig. 8.15). Available in left and right handed forms, it is supplied with

The same small slipstone or diamond slip can be used to tidy up the cutting edges. Ideally, the top surface should be polished to promote easy passage of the chip. At our rates of metal removal this is not critical but it is helpful to ensure the direction of grinding marks is more or less that of the chip.

To set the tool, imagine a square corner cut into the work, one edge along the line of the cut, the other perpendicular to it. Arrange the tool so the tip points into this corner with suitable clearance on both sides. Suitably shaped tools may be used for ordinary or facing cuts at the same setting, although the basic knife tool is happiest cutting along the length of the work. An 8mm (⁵⁄₁₆in) tool will not quite come to centre height, so you can shim it up with one or more little slips of sheet metal. Pieces cut from an aluminium drink can are ideal for this – dull sharp edges and corners with abrasive paper.

One useful variation for the knife tool is to angle it slightly 'backwards' (Fig. 8.13.A). It will not now cut into a square shoulder but it can withstand heavier 'roughing' cuts. A relatively large radius ground on the corner of the tool gives one that can be used for roughing and finishing.

The reward of a sharp and well-set tool, cutting at the ideal depth, feed and speed, is a fine and regular cut. With some materials, especially tough steels or aluminium alloys,

it may also be long, stringy and sharp curls of swarf. While it may be entertaining to see one snake off across the workbench, it is also risky. If one finds its way inside the control box of the lathe it can cause major damage and possibly an electric shock. Worse, long swarf can snag clothing or fingers and then get wound into the machine.

In these cases, grinding a chip breaking groove behind the cutting edge can help. You can use a Dremel type rotary tool with a cutting disk, although doing this may limit how many times you can regrind the tool. An alternative is to clamp a small barrier to the back of the tool or, if cutting speed is modest, to use a hooked piece of stout wire to break the swarf if it gets too long. Never try to pull swarf free with your fingers.

*Fig. 8.15 Left and right handed examples of the Diamond tangential turning tool.*

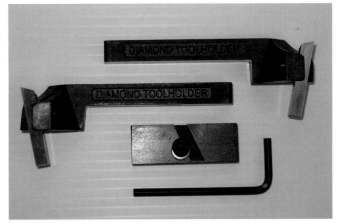

*Fig. 8.16 Facing a large ring with the Diamond tool holder.*

five: left and right hand roughing and knife tools and a boring bar. They may not leave a very good finish but when dealing with very hard or intractable materials, such as some stainless steels or iron castings with a thick 'skin', they let you take a decent cut that gets down to more easily worked metal beneath.

### Indexed Carbide Tools

Indexable tools are a far cry from the tipped tooling, they have precise tool geometry, built-in chip breakers and come in a bewildering range of sizes, shapes and compositions to deal with almost any machining problem. They also have the benefit of coming ready sharpened and with as many as three or four usable corners (Fig. 8.18). Although they can be vulnerable to chipping, especially on interrupted cuts, carbide tools typically keep their edge longer than HSS tools and can be worked harder.

Even so, indexable tooling disappoints many owners of small machine tools. The reason is that most carbide inserts are designed to be worked fast and hard, in some cases so hard the chips are not just blue, but red-hot. They are also designed to take much deeper cuts than hobbyists typically use – on what is intended to be a light finishing cut an indexable tip might merely rub along the surface. A mini-lathe, or indeed most hobby machines, cannot put that much power into the tool tip, yet such inserts are often the ones included in

a sharpening jig and a pair are capable of carrying out most day to day turning operations (Fig. 8.16).

### CARBIDE TOOLING

There are two common types of carbide lathe tool: those with brazed on tips (tipped tools) and those with replaceable tips held in place by a central screw, called indexable tools. On occasion, you may encounter inserted tools that use a small clamp to hold the insert. Solid carbide tools as used in milling are rarely found in lathe work. You might assume all carbide tools are similar but in fact there is a huge variation in their capabilities and suitability.

### Brazed Tip Tools

It is not difficult to find cheap sets of brazed tipped tools, often in bright colours, marketed as suitable for mini-lathes (Fig. 8.17). I have yet to encounter anyone who has been wholly satisfied with these tools. This is not to say you can't get quality tools of this type but the cheap ones often come with poor cutting edges and are difficult to sharpen well (you need to have a green grit wheel and then hone them with a diamond slip). They have little top rake and that makes it hard work for a mini-lathe to get decent results with them even when well finished. That said, it is worth having a small selection of these tools. They usually come in a box of

*Fig. 8.17 An inexpensive set of brazed carbide tools.*

*Fig. 8.18 An indexed carbide cutting tool suitable for mini lathes.*

relatively inexpensive sets of tooling aimed at the hobby market.

The good news is there are tips suitable for use on smaller machines. Two inserts I have been recommended and found suitable for mini-lathe use are CCMT060204 for general use and CCGT060204 for aluminium and stainless steel. These work well with relatively light cuts but can also remove metal at an astonishing rate. If you want to try different inserts, I strongly recommend you take the advice of a specialist supplier.

There is no reason to believe you must have indexable tools or that they are an instant route to better results. Indeed, in many circumstances, especially where you are making light finishing cuts, a sharp HSS tool, especially a tangential tool, will give you the best surface finish. That said, with a couple of indexable tools and a few spare tips in your kit you should have be confident of getting good results in almost any material.

## CARBON STEEL TOOLS

Until the advent of special tool steels such as Mushet, Stellite and modern HSS, all turning of steel was done with hardened and tempered carbon steel tools. It is a little appreciated fact that carbon steel can take a better edge than HSS but it has the disadvantage it easily overheats and 'loses its temper'. It is rare to find carbon steel tools today but if you can source a relatively small, swan-necked, round-nosed, carbon steel tool then grab it! If kept razor sharp and used to take very light cuts, it will be ideal for getting an excellent finish on steel.

The simplicity of hardening carbon steels such as silver steel and gauge plate opens the door to producing our own tools, particularly form tools in special shapes and sizes that may not be available in other materials or will be prohibitively expensive if they are. Silver steel tips can also be silver soldered or even attached with cyano-acrylate adhesive on to mild steel shanks (Fig. 8.19).

*Fig. 8.19 Using a round silver steel cutter glued onto a mild steel shank.*

While some form tools can be made by grinding the end of a piece of HSS tool steel to shape, for more complex shapes an easier way is to shape a piece of gauge plate (or even an annealed piece of an old file). This can done by drilling or filing the profile on the end, then hardening it. In brief, this is done by heating gauge plate to bright red for five minutes per 6mm (¼in) of thickness, then quenching it in oil. The tool should then be polished and reheated (not by a direct flame) until it becomes a dark straw colour, and then be quenched again.

Whatever means you choose to make form tools, ensure they have some front relief so they do not rub the work, as they are liable to chatter because of the lengthy cutting edge. If you use a drill to make a curved edge for a tool, angling the gauge plate at about 10 degrees is an easy way to create such relief. Incorporate some top rake if you can but this is not absolutely essential, especially when working free-cutting materials.

Don't forget the work will show any imperfections in the cutting edge so try to ensure your tool is as sharp and well-finished as possible. You may or may not need to put your form tool in a holder or clamp of some kind but you will need to get it firmly in the toolholder at centre height. The high forces on a form tool mean similar precautions to parting off should be taken,

although you may need to reduce the lathe speed still further, not least to prevent the tool from overheating.

## BORING BARS

As we will see later, boring is in essence just like normal turning but the challenge is, of course, the tool has to fit inside the hole it is making, something complicated slightly by the need for greater front relief to ensure the tool doesn't rub in the hole.

### Inserted Cutter Boring Bars

For larger holes the usual form of boring bar is, quite literally, a hefty bar adapted to hold a cutting tool at the end (Fig. 8.20). As such bars are usually round, they come with suitable holders that facilitate fitting them to a

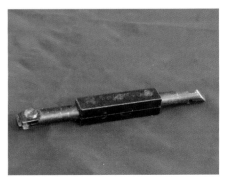

*Fig. 8.20 A boring bar that takes 1/8in (3.2mm) square HSS toolbits.*

normal toolpost. The inserts may be either HSS or carbide. These cutters behave in exactly the same way as other tools but they usually require greater front rake to ensure they don't foul the hole. If the lower part of the cutter isn't clear of the work then the bar simply won't cut. This may not always be obvious as a bar may cut at first and stop as it goes further into the hole and contacts the work.

One advantage of a boring bar that takes HSS bits is you can grind up your own selection of shapes easily so that, as well as boring, the tool can be used for internal grooving and threading, among other uses.

### Solid Boring Bars

For smaller holes it is difficult to make an inserted cutter small enough to fit, although some carbide-tipped boring bars are very small. Fortunately, it becomes more economic to make solid boring bars from HSS and other materials in small sizes.

Broadly speaking, there are two main styles of solid boring bar, usually made from HSS but sometimes in carbide. One type is rather like a knife tool with a reduced shank section and a square body (Fig. 8.21). These can be held in the toolpost like any normal square shanked tool. These tools often have extra material around the head itself but sometimes they suffer from a lack of front relief when used in small holes. With an HSS tool it is relatively easy to grind away some

*Fig. 8.22 Sold for use with boring heads, these boring bars can also be used in the lathe with a suitable holder.*

of the lower corner of the tool, as has been done with the one pictured.

The second style has a round body and the end has a section that is basically a half-cylinder (Fig. 8.22). Although these are often sold as suitable for use with boring heads, they work well held in a suitable holder with a circular bore. The catch with round boring tools is they need to be set at both the correct height and the correct angle, which is usually more or less horizontal and at centre height. This does mean they usually work with very little, if any, top rake.

With either style of tool, the one piece shank is relatively stiff so it can be reduced in section. The reduced shank provides plenty of space for chips to exit the work but if the shank is too slender, the tool will be subject to excessive flexing and vibration, leading to chatter.

### Making a Small Boring Bar

An ideal example of a useful home-made tool is a small boring bar, as bars for really small holes are hard to come by. Fit a suitable piece of mild steel bar, say 10mm (⅜in) square into the toolpost, and, drilling and reaming from the headstock, bore a 6mm (¼in) hole right through, 1.5mm (¹⁄₁₆in) from one side. Now split the thicker side carefully with a hacksaw. It can now be used to clamp a 6mm (¼in) diameter bar when held firmly

in the toolpost, as the clamping screws will close up the block. The centre of such a bar should now be at exactly centre height.

Now take either a 6mm (¼in) diameter HSS toolbit, or a similar piece of silver steel, and grind away just over half of the diameter for a length of about 12mm (½in) then grind across the end at an angle of about 15 to 20 degrees. If using silver steel, harden it and temper to straw. Mounted in the toolpost at an angle of about 7 to 10 degrees, turned so the cutting edge is at centre height, you now have a tool that can enter a hole only slightly larger than its diameter (Fig. 8.23). There is no reason why you can't go even smaller: 5mm (³⁄₁₆in) is quite practical but remember such tools will be quite springy and can therefore take only light cuts. You also have to take care the tool doesn't get

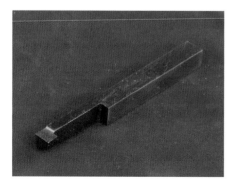

*Fig. 8.21 This boring bar is ground from a single piece of HSS.*

*Fig. 8.23 A boring bar ground from round HSS can enter a hole on slightly larger than the bar itself.*

jammed up with swarf when working in small holes.

## PARTING TOOLS

Parting is one of the most demanding tasks for the lathe. They have to balance being wide enough for rigidity with being narrow enough to minimize the width of the cutting edge. There is always a compromise in this area, creating risks of chatter from either a too-wide cutting edge or a too flexible tool! As the tool works deeper into the groove, the risk of swarf becoming trapped increases and, with it, the danger of a jam.

The classic parting tool is ground on one side (to make it easier to get close to the chuck safely) as a reverse tapered blade (Fig. 8.24). It is often suggested to angle the end to avoid leaving a pip on the work. With thinner parting tools than 3.2mm (⅛in) wide it is best to keep the end straight as otherwise it will tend to flex.

Many parting tools are over size for a mini-lathe (Fig. 8.25) and for delicate work a relatively narrow but short, tool is easier to use and is comfortably stiff enough. The standard tools with 3.2mm (⅛in) wide blades just waste material and invite chatter. Choosing a 2.5mm (³⁄₃₂in) width tool may not seem a big difference but might make a significant difference to you.

*Fig. 8.25 This hefty carbide tipped parting tool is rather over-large for a mini-lathe.*

A favourite parting tool has a deep, parallel sided, blade 1.6mm (¹⁄₁₆in) thick (Fig. 8.26). Ground straight across at the end (to avoid flexing loads), it is quite capable

*Fig. 8.26 Mounted in a quick-change holder, this parting blade is ground down to provide a very thin blade at the reverse end.*

of making parting cuts 19mm (¾in) deep, aided by cutting oil applied by brush. Being supplied as a blade only, it requires a bespoke holder. The tool is constant width, so it is less prone to jamming from swarf dragged down its side but it does need to be aligned carefully.

## TOOL SETTING

In the sections on turning technique you will often see the comment that the tool should be set at centre height. It is self-evident if you are cutting into round work having the tool slightly low or high effectively changes the angle the tool is entering the work, making all the care put into grinding the tool to proper angles somewhat pointless.

If the tool is too high, then the front relief is reduced and it is likely to rub rather than cut. If it is too low, the amount of top rake is effectively decreased. This means the tool has to work harder and has more strain on it. These effects become more marked as the size of the work decreases and sometimes a tool that appears to be working well can start to struggle as the work is turned to a smaller diameter, the opposite of what usually happens with a well-set tool.

Many designs and techniques for tool height setting have been published over the years. I find the easiest technique is to take a very light facing cut across a stub of waste material – you can do this with almost any style of tool, even a parting tool, if the cut is fine enough. If the tool is on centre height then it will not leave a centre pip, too low and there will be an obvious pip, too high the pip will be less marked but you will feel increased resistance as the tool approaches the centre.

Naturally, this is not always possible if you are changing a tool with work already in the chuck. One alternative is to set the tool against the tip of a centre in the tailstock. Probably the most flexible solution is

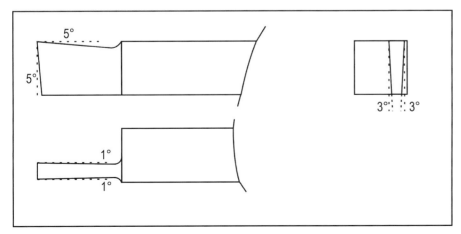

*Fig. 8.24 The angles of a typical parting tool.*

to make a gauge that rests on the lathe bed or the cross slide with a horizontal bar, with its underside at centre height.

## MEASURING EQUIPMENT

A lathe is a precision instrument, capable of working to fine tolerances and accuracies smaller than you can judge by eye. If you are to get the best from your lathe, you need some basic measuring equipment. It isn't essential to have all the following items, a rule and a digital caliper are probably the sensible and economic minimum to get started.

## Rule

Having explained the need for precision measuring equipment, although much of the work you do on the lathe will be to close tolerances, there are plenty of times when you will find a proper engineer's rule invaluable. In the majority of cases smaller is better and a 150mm (6in) rule with both metric and imperial graduations will be suitable for most purposes, from checking the sizes of stock to checking the sizes of components that don't need to be super-accurate in size, such as the depth of locating spigots or the diameter of a knob. They can also be handy for a sense check on things such as screw thread pitches or whether that diameter is 9mm or 10mm?

If you can, get a rule that has a section of close graduations – typically 0.5mm and 0.010in. You may need a loupe or magnifying glass to read them but there will be times this is useful.

One rule you may find particularly useful is to have one only 25mm (1in) long – this can be cut down from a larger cheap rule (Fig. 8.27). You will be surprised how often a little rule that can fit between work and tool speeds things up as you don't have to wind the tool clear from the work and reset it again afterwards.

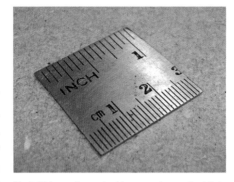

*Fig. 8.27 A very short rule aids measuring work while it is still in the chuck.*

## Caliper

There are two main types of measuring caliper – traditional verniers and digital calipers (Fig. 8.28). Many hobby engineers have a nice pair of vernier calipers and most keep them safe in a drawer as digital ones, with a clear display instead of a complex scale, are so much easier to use. Other advantages of digital calipers are you can zero them at any point, so you can measure how much the size of the work has changed or the difference in size between two objects. With a little ingenuity, you can even use them to measure the movement of the lathe's slides (Fig. 8.29).

*Fig. 8.28 Inexpensive digital calipers are very easy to use.*

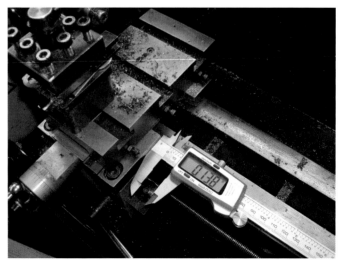

*Fig. 8.29 Using a digital caliper to measure movement of the saddle.*

Typically reading to 0.01mm or 0.0005in, digital calipers are the ideal device for quick checks on the length, diameter or depth of various items. Beware the odd super-economy pair – these are typically in carbon fibre and only read to 0.1mm/0.01in, although a pair of these is handy for non-critical work such as checking stock sizes.

While the outside jaws of calipers will measure external diameters accurately, the internal jaws will slightly under-read the size of a hole, especially a small one, because they are not ground to a knife edge.

You can pay a fortune for an expensive pair of digital calipers but even relatively cheap ones are more than adequate for most lathework. The issues with cheaper calipers are two-fold – some have readings that 'wander' with changes in temperature or can lose their setting over time, the other is the batteries tend to run flat fairly quickly. The answer to the first of these is to always close the caliper and set it to zero before making a measurement. As for the second issue, use quality silver oxide or lithium batteries to ensure a reasonable life.

To get the best out of calipers, make sure the little screw at the back is adjusted so they move smoothly without shake. For critical measurements, squeeze the blades on to the work, rather than pushing on the body of the caliper. This makes it less likely to twist the caliper and get a wrong reading.

It's possible to get hold of left-hand digital calipers. These are much easier to use close to the chuck and it's a surprise they are not more popular.

## Micrometer

If calipers are the ideal day to day measuring tool, reach for a micrometer when you want the next step in precision (Fig. 8.30). Again, digital micrometers are far easier to use than mechanical ones (although most digital 'mikes' also work as mechanical ones).

Most reasonable quality digital micrometers will read to 0.001mm or 0.00005in,

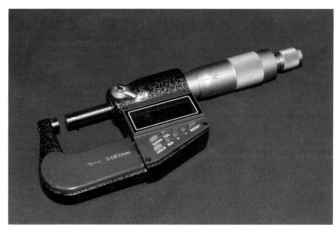

*Fig. 8.30 Like most digital micrometers, this model can also be used as a manual micrometer.*

with an accuracy of two or three times that amount. These are really tiny distances and if you need to be 'spot on' to 0.001mm, then you probably need to buy a very expensive toolroom lathe, not a mini-lathe! The advantage is, of course, that when working to a realistic level of 0.01mm (0.0005in) the greater precision of a micrometer gives us extra confidence.

Typically, micrometers have a relatively limited range of about 25mm (1in) so they are sold in steps of that size (they come with accurately sized bars for setting the larger models). To get accurate results they should be set to zero before use, making sure the faces of the anvils (and the test bar, if required) are scrupulously clean.

Naturally, the higher precision of a micrometer requires greater skill in their use to get accurate results. Some people use the clutch knob on the end of the micrometer, turning it until it makes a set number of clicks, while others rely on developing a 'feel' for closing the mike accurately on the work. I suggest you practise both techniques to see which gives you the most consistent results.

## Dial Gauge

Dial gauges have a 'probe' that can be used to make accurate measurements of small movements (Fig. 8.31). A typical application is to check on the concentricity of work but they can also be used for many other tasks,

*Fig. 8.31 The dial gauge accurately measures the displacement of the plunger.*

such as checking tailstock alignment or measuring small movements of the saddle. Naturally, you can't get useful results using a dial gauge or 'clock' held in the hand, so it is normally held on a hefty stand or one with a magnetic base. This can be attached to the lathe bed, saddle or headstock, for example.

This is one example of a device where the analogue type has more potential than a digital one, as they can be used on a slowly moving surface (such as the outside of rotating work) and the motion of a needle is far easier to interpret than a flickering display.

Usually they have a sensitivity of 0.01mm or 0.0005in but, if checking concentricity, it is often easy to detect 'out of roundness' much less than this by looking for small movements of the needle. For accuracy, it is important to make sure the probe is square-on to the work and it is working on a clean, smooth surface.

## Dial Test Indicator (DTI)

DTIs are typically rather more sensitive than dial gauges but the downside of this is they are a little less robust. They have a small, hinged probe that can be used in the same way as that of a dial gauge, except it needs to be at right angles to the work (Fig. 8.32).

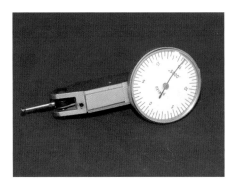

*Fig. 8.32 Dial test indicators (DTIs) detect the angular movement of the probe.*

This very small probe and ability to work at an angle gives them the flexibility to work inside small holes and on other hard to reach surfaces. The downside is that, except for very small distances of say 0.5mm (0.02in), the rules of trigonometry mean it can't make exact measurements. Instead, a DTI is normally used as a comparator, showing movement either side of zero, rather than for absolute measurement.

## OTHER BITS AND PIECES

Everyone has different needs and will have a different view of the other equipment they need around the lathe. The following list just gives a few examples of items you will probably find useful:

◆ A 25mm (1in) paintbrush for clearing away swarf
◆ A 13mm (½in) paintbrush and a pot for neat cutting oil
◆ An old toothbrush for cleaning chucks and other equipment
◆ A scriber and a magic marker for marking out
◆ A depth gauge for checking the depth of holes
◆ Bore gauges (used with a micrometer for measuring the size of holes accurately)
◆ A collection of Allen keys and spanners for adjusting the lathe
◆ Clean rags and kitchen roll (don't use rags near moving parts)
◆ A wooden board to protect the lathe bed if you resort to hacksawing parts held in the chuck
◆ One or more magnetic bases for holding the DTI, guards, etc
◆ Various small pieces of sheet metal (bits of drinks cans are good) for shimming tools to centre height
◆ Some $\frac{5}{16}$in square HSS for making toolbits (you will also need a grinder!)
◆ Safety goggles.

# 9 Basic Turning

## A TRIAL CUT

Before starting a project in earnest it's a good idea to make a few 'practice' parts to familiarize yourself with the lathe. It's not just how fast things move but what direction they go in!

For your first practice piece, I suggest you choose a bar of an easily turned metal such as brass, aluminium or free-cutting mild steel (which is considerably cheaper). A bar around 20mm (¾in) diameter is a good size. If it is a standard 300mm (12in) bar, I suggest you cut it down to no more than 150mm (6in) long as you can then practise on it without the need for tailstock support. If you have to use a smaller diameter bar, reduce the length.

Fit the three-jaw chuck to the lathe. Making sure bar and chuck are clean, clamp the bar in the chuck, ensuring the clamped end is supported along the full length of the chuck jaws. Tighten it up securely but don't overtighten as the chuck key is designed for single-handed use.

Now fit a suitable tool in the toolpost. As explained in the previous chapter, it should be sharp and at centre height. A knife tool is ideal or you could use a general tool from one of the standard toolkits. Make sure the top slide is set in the normal position. Make sure the direction selector at the back of the headstock is at neutral and the gear selector is in the 'low' position.

Move the slides so the tool's tip is aligned with but is not quite touching the outer tip of the metal bar (Fig. 9.1). As the leadscrew drive is in neutral, engage the clasp nuts using the lever on the apron. This will stop the saddle from moving. Check both tool and work are secure and put on a pair of safety goggles – swarf will soon be flying!

Switch on the lathe and unclip the emergency stop button. You can now use the variable speed control to increase the speed of the lathe gradually until it is spinning at a modest rate.

Using the cross slide handle, advance the tool slowly until it just touches the work. This is easier to hear than see. One approach (when working to fine limits) is to put a wet cigarette paper on the work. The tool tip will tear the paper away when it is roughly 0.025mm (0,001in) from the metal.

Stop the lathe with the e-stop button. You will probably see the tool has marked the bar but only on part of its circumference. This is because three-jaw chucks rarely hold work perfectly concentrically. Set the cross slide index to zero, now wind the tool back a half-turn so it is clear of the bar and move it over beyond the right end of the bar.

Now 'put on the cut'. Start by moving the tool forward so the index returns to zero – this is more or less the surface of the bar. Advance the tool another ten graduations. This sets it for a cut of 0.25mm (0.010in). Start the lathe and bring it up to speed. An ideal speed for mild steel of this size is about 300rpm. For brass you could go a fair bit faster, say 500rpm, but this is not essential and a lower speed may help your confidence.

Using the top slide handwheel, advance the tool sideways gently towards the work. A rate of about one turn per second will give you a chip thickness of (60sec × 40 division/500 rpm) or about five scale divisions – 0.125mm (0.005in). The tool will enter the work and, depending on the tool and the metal, you will either see a long coil of swarf start to 'peel' off the work or get a

Fig. 9.1 Everything ready for a first try at turning.

succession of smaller pieces of swarf, which will be a multitude of tiny ones in the case of brass. If it's long, stringy swarf remember NOT to try to remove it with your hand – you could end up losing a finger. Instead, use a length of stout wire with a hook on the end. Keep the cut up until you have covered a good 50mm (2in) or more of the bar, then retract the tool with the cross slide and stop the lathe and inspect your work. If the cut has not covered the full circumference of the bar, repeat the exercise.

If you have used decent tools and free-cutting metal you should have achieved a reasonable finish. If it isn't perfect, as your technique becomes more practised and smoother, the finish will improve. Practise taking more turning cuts, in particular try turning up to a shoulder by cutting repeatedly up to a particular reading along the work, increasing the depth of cut each time. If you are cutting steel, using some neat cutting oil (applied by brush) will help improve the finish and extend the life of the edge of your cutting tools.

If you have a micrometer or a pair of measuring calipers (digital ones are inexpensive and easier to use) see if you can set yourself a target dimension and cut the metal exactly to it. Note that on normal cuts, feeding the tool in by any amount results in twice that much coming off the diameter (with facing cuts the length change is the same as the amount of feed).

Experiment with different depths of cut but take care with deeper cuts not to strain the lathe or the motor. Note how, if you take a more generous cut, say fifteen divisions (0.375mm or 0.015in) and then pass the tool over the work at the same setting again, it will take a further fine shaving cut. This is because the cutting forces act to push the tool away from the work. You need to allow for this when getting close to final size – taking that second cut is often called 'working the spring out of the tool' and it is wise to make such a second pass before taking a final fine cut.

Try making finer cuts. See how small a cut you can take. With a sharp HSS tool you may be able to make a very fine cut of just half a division (0.015mm or 0.0005in), which is about the limit for a mini-lathe with standard tools. When you try to turn to an exact size it helps if you try to make sure the final cut will be fairly small but not tiny, say about four divisions (0.10mm or 0.004in). This minimizes the spring in the tool but is enough to ensure a proper cut, rather than just scraping the work.

Disengage the feed nuts and try putting on a cut using the handwheel instead of the top slide. You will have to take it gently as the handwheel moves the saddle much faster and with less control. It's worth practising though, as when you get the feel for this technique it is the fastest and most convenient way to remove a lot of metal rapidly.

Don't be afraid to try different speeds. As the metal gets thinner, try faster speeds. Get used to how you have to slow down the federate if the lathe is running more slowly. Pay attention to how freely the tool is cutting. If it starts to struggle, take a close look at it under a lens as it may be getting blunt. A quick touch up with a slipstone or diamond slip should sort out any minor loss of the edge on the tool.

Once you have reduced your bar to a short, thin, many shouldered rod and a

surprisingly large pile of swarf – congratulations! You have started on the long but satisfying road to becoming a proficient turner. There will be setbacks along the way but the simple pleasure of seeing a clean, well-finished part emerge from the raw material will never go away.

## Depth of Cut

If you refer to your mini-lathe manuals seeking advice on appropriate depths of cut, you may well be disappointed. Some of them quote a very conservative 0.25mm (0.010in) depth of cut, while others discreetly avoid mentioning the subject. Presumably this is because there are so many variables at work, the manufacturers don't want to risk giving advice that could result in the lathe being overloaded.

In truth, with good tools, neat cutting oil and a little care you should be able to take significantly deeper cuts under the right circumstances.

A mini-lathe in good condition is quite capable of cuts of 1mm (0.040in) or more in free-cutting mild steel such as 230m07 (also known as EN1a) at a diameter of 25mm (1in). In soft metals such as aluminium or brass, deeper cuts can be taken. Fig. 9.2 shows the results of taking a 2mm (0.080in) depth of cut in 1in diameter mild steel on a standard

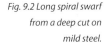

*Fig. 9.2 Long spiral swarf from a deep cut on mild steel.*

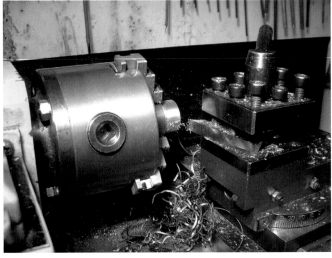

mini-lathe. To achieve this the lathe does need to be well set up and the tool sharp. For most work, 2mm is probably a sensible maximum depth of cut, although a 500W brushless motor lathe has been tested at a 2.3mm DOC. With tough materials such as higher carbon steels or stainless steels, depths of cut will be smaller, sometimes much smaller.

To achieve decent depths of cut you do need well-formed and sharp tools, and to use the right speed. You also need to appreciate at larger diameters you will have less torque and may need to reduce the depth of cut to avoid stalling the machine.

One of the skills of turning is to learn how your own machine behaves under different circumstances. If you find it is cutting easily and freely, and the motor is not noticeably slowing when the cut starts, you may well be able to increase the depth of cut. If the motor labours at all, the overload light illuminates or a fuse or circuit breaker blows, then you are certainly trying to make too deep a cut.

Learn to use your eyes and ears to monitor how the lathe is cutting. Are you getting nice, regular swarf or is it ragged and uneven? Is the tool 'chattering' or screeching? Use your fingers as well – if the slides are well adjusted you will feel feedback through the handles of the lathe that will let you know if the tool is struggling. It's particularly important to keep alert for the deterioration in ease of cutting (and surface finish) caused by the tool blunting, chipping or having a build-up of material on its tip. If this happens the best thing to do is stop the cut and give the tool a little attention.

So, start with modest cuts of about 0.25mm (0.010in) but as you develop your skills don't be afraid to experiment with deeper cuts.

## FEEDS AND SPEEDS

When cutting materials there are several things to bear in mind. Firstly, there is the material itself, which means allowing for not just its hardness and toughness but also for the way in which it cuts. Secondly, there is the type of tool being used. Carbide tooling is designed to work much faster than HSS.

The aspects you can control are the cutting speed or how fast the tool moves across the work, usually given in metres or feet per minute. This is dependent on both the diameter of the work and the rotational speed of the lathe.

A second factor is the feed rate, or how far the tool moves along the work for each rotation, and the third is the depth of cut. For mini-lathes, the slowest automatic feed is 0.01mm (0.004in) per revolution and a typical depth of cut for general work is 1mm (0.01in).

There is no great merit in a faster feed rate, except in very easily cut materials such as aluminium, and although you can vary the depth of cut it is likely not to be more than 2mm. You have greatest control over the speed of the lathe and this is the area that creates the most confusion.

One problem is that many books and websites quote cutting speeds that have been calculated for industrial situations where tool life is balanced against production speed and the lathes are usually much bigger and more powerful. This creates problems for beginners who look up their material and a cutting speed only to find they have poor results, their tool rapidly blunts and the results get even worse.

The chart (Fig. 9.3) gives suggested speeds for HSS tools for various diameters of work and a number of the most commonly encountered metals. Carbide tools can be run about twice as fast, remembering the best results will be achieved with inserts designed for use on small machines. For material significantly less than 10mm in diameter, double the 10mm speed or, if this is above top speed, run the lathe as fast as it will go. For larger work, slow the lathe in proportion (Fig. 9.4). Be aware running the lathe at low rpm, even in low gear, for an extended period will lead to overheating.

With variable speed it is easy to change the speed of the lathe and even speed up as the diameter of the work is reduced but in all honesty the best guide to correct speed is not this chart – it is just a guide, a starting point. Pay more attention to how the tool behaves – does it cut smoothly and leave a good finish or does it chatter or shriek, or leave a finish like a ploughed field? You won't get good results with a poor tool but even a good tool will let you know if it is 'unhappy' and you may find tweaking the speed up or down can give much better results.

### Spindle Speed Readouts

Some mini-lathes are fitted with readouts giving the spindle speed in revolutions per minute (rpm), while others have a socket allowing a readout to be fitted and there are various designs for shop-made readouts. These will all enable you to achieve fine control of spindle speed in combination with the variable speed control. In truth, however, just as with depth of cut, the best guides to the right speed for any situation are your senses. This is particularly true for demanding tasks such as parting off or using form tools. Nonetheless, a speed readout can be a reassurance and a useful guide, even for the more experienced lathe user.

## CUTTING FLUIDS

The finish and ease of machining most metals can be improved by the use of cutting fluids. The exceptions to this are those metals that break up readily into a stream of fine chips, rather than producing true swarf – that is cast iron and most brasses.

There are two main types of cutting fluid – soluble oils and neat cutting oils. Soluble cutting oils are used in a highly diluted form, more usually a stable emulsion than a true solution. Applied as a flood, they lubricate

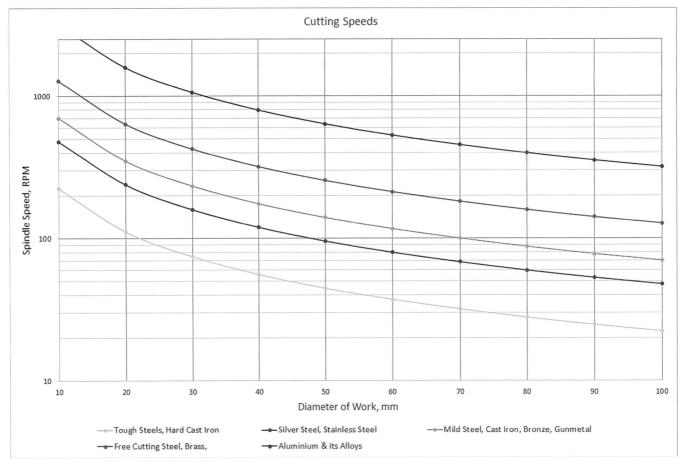

## Cutting Speeds

Fig. 9.3 Suggested speeds for cutting different materials.

Fig. 9.4 Turning the outside of a large ring with a 'Diamond' tangential tool.

the cutting area, wash away swarf and act as a coolant – an excellent combination of properties. Unfortunately, even with anti-fungal and anti-corrosion additives, they do have a number of shortfalls for the occasional and small lathe user. For a start, you need a closed circuit system that collects and filters the used coolant and pumps it back to the cutting point. Then a generous flow of coolant can end up being sprayed around the workshop and you need to clean up scrupulously at the end of each session unless the lathe is in almost continuous use to avoid corrosion. Also, coolant left to stand can become pretty unpleasant and there are also serious health hazards associated with inhaling any overspray. This is not to say many people do not enjoy considerable success in using soluble cutting oils – just that doing so is not straightforward.

Neat cutting oils are very different and act largely as a lubricant (they may have modest cooling properties when used for relatively slow processes including tapping). No complex system is required as it is possible to apply the oil by brush or as a gentle drip-feed (Fig. 9.5). There are still the hazards of

Fig. 9.5 Taking a cut using neat cutting oil.

flinging the oil around if the lathe is run fast, or of unpleasant smoke if the tool or work overheat, but most of the benefits of improved finish and reduced cutting forces can be enjoyed through the use of neat cutting oil.

Cost wise, neat cutting oil is more expensive but a litre bottle, applied by brush (Fig. 9.6), will last a long time. It can also be used to improve results when tapping, reaming, milling or drilling by hand, or with other machine tools. Any surplus on the brush can be applied to the lathe's slides, leadscrew and so on to help keep them lubricated.

which can greatly improve the machining of aluminium and its alloys.

## CUTTING WITH POWER FEED

Once you are able to take a cut along the outside of a bar confidently, you will probably start to notice the finish is not as smooth and even as you might like. You will also notice you can usually improve it by moving the tool across the work relatively slowly and very evenly. The good news is the lathe can do this automatically for you! The mechanism is known as power feed or 'self

act' and works by linking the saddle to the leadscrew and turning the latter relatively slowly (Fig. 9.7).

The first step is to isolate the lathe from the mains, remove the gear cover and set up the gearbox for fine feed, using the steel 20-tooth pinions and the two largest (80-tooth) changewheels (Fig. 9.8). These provide a reduction gear of 16:1 between the mandrel and the leadscrew. As the leadscrew is 1.5mm or 1/16in pitch, this gives a feed of about 0.1mm or 0.004in – near enough the same whether you have a metric or imperial leadscrew. Start by fitting a 20-tooth wheel on to the fixed wheel below the reversing gear, taking care not to lose the small metal 'key' that tacks it to the spindle.

Next, fit a 20- and 80-tooth pair of wheels to the sleeve that fits over the stud on the 'banjo', again being careful to keep track of the key. The 80-tooth gear goes on the inside. You will need to loosen the nut at the back of the stud and slide it along the banjo, as well as loosening the nut that keeps the banjo in place. Leave them both loose for now. The last gear is an 80-tooth one on the end of the leadscrew. Note the small metal collar should be fitted over the key and on the inside of the gear. You may need to engage the leadscrew feed nuts

Fig. 9.7 The clasp nuts engage the leadscrew and move the saddle along the bed.

Fig. 9.6 A coarse bristle brush is ideal for applying cutting oil.

There are other fluids that can be used to aid the machining of different metals. Perhaps the most useful is paraffin (kerosene) applied by brush, *not* as a flood,

Fig. 9.8 This gear train is set up for fine feed.

Fig. 9.9 In forward gear, the tumbler reverse engages only the larger (white) idler gear.

Fig. 9.11 In reverse, the drive passes through both idler gears.

Fig. 9.10 For neutral, neither gear is engaged.

on the saddle apron to stop the leadscrew rotating.

Finally, you need to mesh the gears in two stages. First, slide the stud along the banjo until the 20-tooth one of the paired gears meshes with the 80-tooth gear on the leadscrew and tighten its nut. A good tip is to nip a piece of paper between the gears to ensure you don't fit them together too tightly. Now swing up the banjo until the 80-tooth gear in the pair meshes with the 20-tooth gear you fitted to the bottom of the reversing arrangement, and lock the banjo in place.

The direction lever at the back of the headstock can now be moved to the forward (or reverse) position to select the direction of feed (Figs 9.9, 9.10 and 9.11). Forward moves the saddle towards the headstock. Make sure the length of the leadscrew and the lathe bed itself are oiled lightly. With the power off, engage the half nuts using the lever on the apron and turn the spindle of the lathe by hand. The saddle should move very slowly along the bed. If all is OK, you can put the direction lever in 'neutral', fit the gearbox cover and reconnect the lathe to the mains. You are now ready to use power

feed and reap the rewards in terms of a fine, smooth finish (Fig. 9.12).

This may all seem a great deal of palaver but it does get easier with practice, and anyway you will find you leave the lathe set

up like this for most of the time. Only when you do some screwcutting will you need to change the gears. In normal use you will simply leave the direction lever in 'neutral', switching it to forward or reverse on the occasions when you need power feed. Don't rely on the saddle feed nuts to disengage the feed when you are not using it – they can drop in unexpectedly, causing all sorts of problems. Imagine engaging power feed by accident in the middle of parting off!

Set up a length of round bar, ideally supported by the tailstock, for a simple lengthwise test cut. Free cutting mild steel would be the ideal material to practise on as it is cheap and relatively easy to cut. Leave the tool not quite touching the work and just past its right hand end. Put the direction

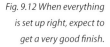

Fig. 9.12 When everything is set up right, expect to get a very good finish.

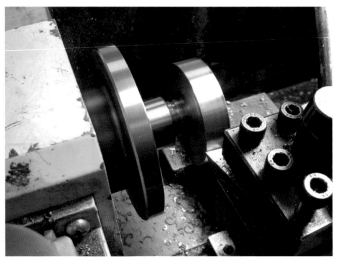

lever into the forward position, make sure the saddle feed nuts are disengaged and start the lathe at a fairly low speed. Take a breath and push down on the apron lever to engage the feed nuts. The saddle will start to move towards the headstock, hopefully at a gentle pace. To stop the saddle instantly, just lift the apron lever. Practise, increasing the lathe speed to normal cutting speeds, until you are confident you can stop the tool wherever you want.

Now stop the lathe and return the tool just past the end of the work with the apron handwheel and apply a cut of 0.10 to 0.15mm (0.004in–0.006in). Start the lathe and engage the apron lever and half nuts. Keep your hand on the lever and watch as the lathe puts on a steady cut, generating clean, even swarf and, hopefully, leaving a nice finish. Don't forget to stop the cut before you reach the chuck or any driving dog! Now, try putting on a second cut – with such a small cut it won't be a disaster if you overrun the end of the first cut but try not to. When you get experienced, you may well turn right up to a shoulder under power feed but it is normal practice to disengage the feed nuts before the tool reaches the end of the cut, and tweak the handwheel to take off the last millimetre or so.

If, instead of a finishing tool, you had made these cuts with a pointed tool, you would have made a very, very fine screw thread on the work. When we come to screwcutting, you will find this is done in exactly the same way but the gears are chosen so the tool moves much faster. Get used to turning under power feed and when you come to try screwcutting under power you will already have learned the instinctive control of the apron lever that will make the task rather less daunting.

A few things to remember about power feed are to always use the direction lever to disengage the power feed securely when not in use and never to leave the lathe unat-tended under power feed, even for a few moments.

## FACING

Now you have mastered nailed turning by hand and under power, set up a shorter and perhaps larger diameter bar in the chuck and try your hand at facing. A piece 25mm (1in) diameter and 35mm (1½in) long is ideal and will suit a spindle speed of about 350rpm.

In principle, facing is a relatively simple machining exercise with the tool just being moved across the face of the work using the cross slide. It's rarely quite that simple though and there are a few things to watch to ensure you get a good, flat, finely finished surface, rather than something that looks like a 78rpm record or has a surface finish like grandma's knitting!

The first requirement is a suitable tool. Bear in mind this will be moving left to right (relative to face of the work), so an ideal choice is a left-handed knife tool, a mirror image of a normal right-handed tool, and mounted along the axis of the lathe. Many indexable tools are designed for turning and facing without a tool change (Fig. 9.13). In practice, the angles of a normal right-handed knife tool will often allow it to be used for satisfactory facing, especially with free cutting materials. If you do this it helps if the tool has a rounded tip rather than a sharp point and it must be set so the tool-

holder can move past the face of the work without fouling it.

Make sure the tool is set at centre height – too low and you will leave a 'pip' on the work, too high and the last bit of cutting will be hard work and you may get an odd shaped dimple in the centre.

To get a good flat face, make sure you lock the saddle in place. The easy way is to ensure the change gears are disengaged (lever at back left of the headstock) and then engage the half nuts. Use the handwheel to move the saddle to the right enough to take up any slack and use the top slide to put on the cut. Note, it is perfectly normal for lathes to face very slightly concave. This is because you can place a concave surface on a flat one (or another concave one) without wobble. A convex surface will wobble on a flat surface.

Use the top slide to bring the tool level with the end of the bar. If the bar is sawn and has an angled end, align with the very furthest point. Zero the top slide index (see Fig. 9.14) and move the tool back towards the headstock by ten divisions of the top slide index. Start the lathe, and this time use the cross slide handle to take a cut across the end of the bar.

To actually make the cut, feed the tool slowly and smoothly across the work. As mini-lathes don't have power cross feed, this

*Fig. 9.13 Facing across the end of a bar – the circular marks cannot be felt with the fingertip.*

*Fig. 9.14 The top slide dial set to zero.*

*Fig. 9.15 Grip the handle so you can apply steady, balanced turning force.*

*Fig. 9.16 Taking a deep facing cut with a knife tool.*

is usually done manually. Use both hands on the handle with a 'balanced grip' (Fig. 9.15) to avoid a 'dead spot' and wind the cross slide in as steadily as you can. Keep it slow to avoid creating a visible spiral groove. In an ideal world, you can speed up the spindle speed as the diameter decreases and up the feed rate to match but, in practice, most of us don't have a sufficient number of hands for such an exercise.

If you are lucky and have a bar with the end already straight this should result in a nice clean facing cut right across. It is more likely the bar has an angled end and the first cut will only tidy up a small section of the bar end so keep repeating the cuts, advancing the cut by ten divisions each time, until the bar has a smooth finish right across.

Once you have cut right across there shouldn't be a central pip. If there is, the tool

is set slightly too low (by half the diameter of the pip). On the other hand, if the tool is set too high, you should feel greatly increased resistance as it rubs past the middle of the work. Why not make cuts deliberately with the tool a little too low or high and see how it affects the 'feel' of the cut and the appearance of the finished surface. Leave this piece in the lathe, as you can use it to practise boring next.

As with turning, reversing the tool out quickly will spoil the finish on a faced surface so wind the top slide back or move the saddle to the right before retracting the tool. One final point: speeds and depths of cut for facing are essentially the same as for normal turning and it is possible to take quite deep facing cuts, even using a knife tool set for normal turning (Fig. 9.16).

### Improving Finish

One way of getting a very good finish, and one that also applies to using the top slide to make a cut, is to use a handheld battery drill or screwdriver set to a slow speed to drive the handwheel. This is easy to do as all that is needed is a 5mm hex bit to fit the handle securing cap screw. Naturally, slopping a brushful of neat cutting oil on the end of the bar will also help with getting a good finish.

### Facing Large Work

You may find you struggle to position the tool so you can face across the whole of a larger workpiece. It may be you need to fit a tool in the front or rear of the tool-holder, or even sticking out at an angle, to reach all the surface you want to face. A little patience and ingenuity should solve these issues. The only really big problem is if you want to face something approaching the lathe's full capacity of 175mm (7in) diameter, such as truing up a faceplate. You are likely to discover the cross slide travel is rather less than half this. There is a simple modification to address this given towards the end of this book.

Obviously, you can only face right across the end of a workpiece if it is unsupported at the tailstock end. If a normal or rotating centre is fitted, then you will end up with a frustrating 'collar' left around the centre, even if you use a fine pointed and cranked tool designed for facing into small spaces. There are three solutions to this. Small diameter work can often be moved back into the chuck, so it projects less, and the facing done as a final operation, especially if this is a cosmetic need rather than a precision operation. If the work is relatively rigid, you can remove the support and, working gently and at reduced speed, carefully face off the collar. For a long thin workpiece, however, this may not be possible or safe to do. In such cases, the solution is something called a 'half centre' – this allows much better access to the end of the work, especially if the centre hole is a good 5mm (³⁄₁₆in) diameter, allowing the half centre to go right in.

## BORING

Boring is effectively 'internal turning' and is quite distinct from drilling, reaming and other methods that use the tool itself to 'size' the hole. These will be dealt with separately. Boring normally means using a single-point tool to take successive cuts, just as you would with ordinary turning, but because the tool is 'inside' the work it is rather less straightforward (Fig. 9.17). On the positive side, boring done well produces very accurate holes.

It is very difficult, and rather slow, to bore a hole from scratch. Indeed, many boring bars will refuse to make any significant impact on a flat surface. The usual approach is first to drill as large a hole as is practical. This has two advantages: it is generally quicker and it allows the use of the largest possible boring bar. The bigger the boring bar, the stiffer it is, the more accurate the hole will be and the better the surface finish. The hole has

to be large enough to allow the boring tool to enter without rubbing. If it can rub, even a little, the hole produced will be far from accurate. It's easy to be caught out because many boring tools will rub *below the cutting edge,* rather than at the back, if the hole is too small, and this may not be obvious as the cause of your bell-mouthed hole.

On the whole, boring bars are less rigid than comparable external turning tools due to their smaller cross-section and the need for them to have sufficient overhang to operate inside a deep hole (Fig. 9.18). One consequence of this is, when finishing a hole, it is usual to make several repeat cuts at the same setting to work out any spring in the tool. Without this, it is quite likely you will end up with a tapered hole. Unless the tool you are using has a round tip and cuts freely in both directions, it is worth making sure it is moved out of contact with the work when being brought out of the hole and returned to the same setting for each repeat cut. You will hear the tool chatter loudly as it reaches the bottom of the hole if you move it too far. Ears, eyes and fingers all play a part in getting it right. Never 'whip' the tool back out of the bored hole without retracting it as this will leave a deep spiral scratch that may affect the next few passes of the tool.

Boring is much easier if the set-up allows the tool to pass right through the work. If the

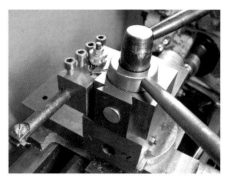

Fig. 9.18 A medium sized boring bar held in a quick change toolpost.

work is held in a chuck or on the faceplate and can be spaced slightly from the chuck/faceplate body then you can see the bar emerge at the end of the cut and stop the lathe before any damage is done. Wind the tool away from you (the opposite to normal) and clear it from the work, then move it back towards you to take the next cut.

Assuming you left the facing test piece in the lathe, move it outwards in the jaws by about 6mm (¼in). This gap is to give a space for the tip of the boring tool to move into without damaging the chuck.

Use a centre drill in a tailstock chuck followed by a reasonably small drill to create a hole right through it. Repeat with slightly larger sizes of drill up to about 12 or 13mm (½in). Some neat cutting fluid and regular clearing of chips will help make this straightforward.

If you have one of the standard sets of mini-lathe tools, it should include a small boring bar. These are suitable for use in holes 12mm (½in) or more in diameter. The tool should be mounted pointing along the length of the lathe bed, as always with the tip at the centre height of the lathe. If you set the tip so it doesn't quite touch the work, it's a good idea to ensure it can be moved right through to the other side of the work without fouling the work. You may need to angle the tool slightly if it does. If the tool isn't quite long enough to reach right through the work without the toolpost fouling the outside of the work, you can use

Fig. 9.17 Boring a steam engine cylinder made from a cast iron bar.

your new facing skills to shorten it until the tool can go right through.

Unlike turning, the tool needs to be moved towards the operator to increase the depth of cut, so retract the cross slide until the tip of the tool just touches the inside wall of the drilled hole. As the hole may not be perfectly central, it is a good idea to make the first cut a very shallow one. Succeeding cuts can be deeper but, as small boring tools are rather flexible, keep the depth of cut to no more than 0.25mm (0.010in) or less.

You need to watch carefully as you take the boring cuts – stop as soon as the tool emerges into the gap between the work and the chuck body. You will hear the cut end before you see the tool.

The greater flexibility of the boring tool and the build up of swarf in the bore means you may find it harder to get a good finish. You will also notice the effect of spring in the tool is much greater, so more than one extra pass may be needed to 'work out the spring'. The answer to this is to clear all swarf out of the hole with a brush between cuts, apply neat cutting oil to the cut and to use fine cuts for finishing.

A good test of your boring skills is to turn a piece of round bar to an exact size, then try to make a bore that is a good, close push fit on it. If you can do this, you are really starting to build your skills.

### Blind Holes

A regular challenge is boring a blind hole (Fig. 9.19). Firstly, you need a boring tool that can cut up to a shoulder – not all boring bars allow this, especially those with inserted HSS cutters, although some double-ended bars will hold an angled cutter for blind holes (Fig. 9.20). Secondly, unless the boring tool is inserted to exactly the same amount each time, there is a good chance it will dig in at the bottom of the hole, causing chatter or even damaging the tool. One solution is to use the top slide to put on the cut and watch the index dial closely. An easier approach

Fig. 9.19 Boring a blind hole in an alloy casting.

is to use a saddle stop, giving maximum repeatability with the least chance of error. If auto feed is used, it should be disengaged just before the saddle contacts the stop and the final bit of feed made by hand. This eliminates any possibility of 'nudging' the stop along the bed. Another option is a mark on the shank of the boring tool. The ability to 'sight' across the end of the work to the mark accurately is not a difficult skill to acquire.

Ideally, the tool used for a blind hole should have minimal end relief so the bottom of the hole is effectively finished almost flat. However, even if you have been very careful, the base of your hole will be left as a series of concentric ridges. Most tool geometries will allow you to make a small cut on the 'back' of the tool. Once the hole is

cut to depth, wind the tool gently away from you and let it skim off all these ridges, like a facing tool. Some tools don't like this and in these cases you will need to note all the readings for the 'inside corner' of the hole and use the boring tool to take an outward cut from the middle of the hole.

### PARTING

Parting off is the action of plunging a narrow tool into the work, effectively creating a groove that ultimately reaches to the centre (or any central hole) and the work literally parts company with the rest of the stock (Fig. 9.21). Parting is one of the most demanding tasks for any lathe. The parting tool has to operate in a deep, narrow groove

Fig. 9.20 Using an angled inserted tool for a blind hole.

Fig. 9.21 Parting off a length of bar.

and this creates several problems, and not just for beginners. Some old hands reach guiltily for the hacksaw rather than part off a large diameter piece of work. The tool has to cut across its whole width and has a large overhang – combined together this is a recipe for chatter and increases the risk of the tool 'digging in'. The swarf can struggle to escape from the groove and, unless lubricant is applied as a substantial jet, it may not reach the tool point.

Even so, parting off need not be a nerve-racking experience, as long as you follow a number of points:

1. A well-adjusted lathe means ensuring the saddle, cross slide and top slide all move smoothly but without any trace of shake or movement. The lathe slides should all be lubricated and in good adjustment. These two points won't just make parting easier, they will help you get better results from all your turning. Rock the toolpost and watch anywhere two slides rub together – if you see a bead of oil moving in and out then they are probably too loose.

2. The spindle bearings should be adjusted properly, without any play or shake. It is easier to get good results with roller bearings fitted but even lathes with deep groove roller bearings can part off successfully. Put a bar in the chuck and pull it back and forth. If there is play, cautiously tighten the lock nuts at the rear of the mandrel a little and test again.

3. The tool should be freshly sharpened. If the finish of the edge is the slightest bit suspect, hone it sharp with a diamond slip.

4. Two essential pieces of advice from George Thomas – one of the past masters of home workshop technique – are to match the size of the tool to the job and to keep the end of the tool square to the job. The parting tool should be relatively narrow. Parallel-sided HSS tools of 1.6mm (¹⁄₁₆in) are good for smaller diameters but 2.5mm (³⁄₃₂in) tools with side relief are more rigid for larger diameter work. Avoid the common advice to angle the end of the tool to prevent it leaving an end pip. This produces sideways forces that can bend the tool off line and jam the job.

5. The cutting edge should be on centre height and the tool exactly at right angles to the work.

6. Start cutting with a speed no more than a third less than you would normally use at the full diameter of the work. Be prepared to tweak the speed up or down if you start to hear chatter.

7. Apply neat cutting oil directly into the cut. One way is with a brush held in your left hand throughout the cut.

8. Don't be afraid of the job. A jam up and a broken tool tip can understandably make you cautious. George Thomas was adamant a confident and positive approach was essential and that over-cautious pecking at the work would never bring good results. Many dig-ins are caused by feeding the tool in gingerly so it is barely cutting. This means it rapidly wears and becomes blunt, the cutting force increases to compensate, then suddenly the tool gets a grip of the work and. . .

Brass is the ideal material for practising your parting off technique. This is not just because it is a relatively free-cutting material but also because its swarf comes off as small chips so it is much less likely to clog up the narrow parting cut. Parting off is much easier with smaller diameters, so begin with modestly sized stock. Choose a relatively short length of brass bar, say 20mm (¾in) diameter by 50mm (2in) long, and practise parting off very thin slices. If you can get the hang of this, check your tool is sharp and have a try on a similarly sized length of free-cutting mild steel.

Finally, there will be times when for one reason or another you do have to reach for

*Fig. 9.22 A wooden bed protector is simple to make and will avoid the disaster of damaging the lathe bed if cutting off work with a hacksaw.*

the hacksaw. Please make a simple wooden protector, just a piece of board with a tenon to fit in the centre of the lathe bed will do, and then you won't end up spoiling the lathe with sawcuts (Fig. 9.22).

## GROOVING

Grooving is essentially just the first step in parting. Typically, most grooves rarely need to be much deeper than they are wide. As they are shallow, you are less likely to encounter problems caused by clogging with swarf or the tool dragging on the sides of the cut. For 'square' grooves, a normal parting tool will suffice but for rounded grooves a suitably shaped tool is needed (Fig. 9.23). If you need a wide, shallow groove, just make repeated overlapping cuts to the

*Fig. 9.23 This long round-nosed tool was made for truing up crankshaft journals but can also be used to make O-ring grooves.*

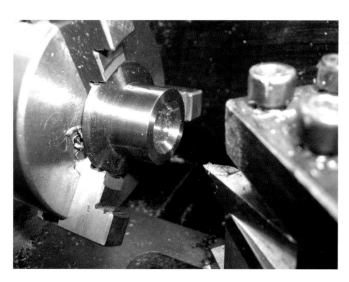

*Fig. 9.24 Chamfering an internal corner by taper turning.*

same depth, aiming to finish no more than 0.05mm (0.002in) short of full depth. Make the last cut to full depth and then traverse the cutter to 'save off' the last bit of metal. Even a relatively narrow tool should be able to cope with a shallow sideways cut like this, as long as you take things gently.

## CHAMFERING

Where a turned and a faced surface meet, the resulting 90 degree corner is typically rather sharp and is unacceptable for parts that are to be handled. Also, it is almost impossible to get paint to cover sharp corners. Chamfering is simply the process of taking off such a sharp corner with an angled cut. It's possible to do this by taper turning (Fig. 9.24) but as most chamfers are not critical, it's easiest just to use a suitably angled tool. The angled cutting edge is just advanced a short way against the corner and a neat chamfer is produced.

An ideal chamfering tool has a 90 degree point (that is 45 degrees either side) and has a top rake angled away from the cutting edge but obviously you potentially need a number of tools for chamfering different corners of the work. A simple solution is a tool ground to have a 45 degree point on the end and with a bit of top rake sloping back from the point. Such a tool can be used to chamfer right or left hand corners and, if set to point along the axis of the lathe, can also chamfer the corners of bored or drilled holes.

In many cases, you will find yourself taking simple shortcuts – an obvious one being rotating the toolpost to present a suitable tool edge at a suitable angle. This is a quite acceptable practice as chamfering cuts are light, as long as you make sure the arrangement doesn't create the risk of a clash between tools and rotating parts.

A more contentious alternative is to use a file to take off the sharp edge (arris) of a turned part. Special files are available that are designed with teeth that tend to push the file to the right and away from the chuck. As you probably won't have one of these files, if you choose to use ordinary files then you will have to take plenty of care. In particular, ensure the file has a big fat handle fitted to protect you if it should be thrown or pushed hard away from the work. Don't make the mistake of thinking small 'needle' files are safer. A needle file without a handle that hits a chuck jaw can easily be forced right into the palm of your hand. Also, be aware the files with 'plastic dipped' handles are not safe to use in this way as the handle can be pushed easily through the plastic coating.

Another, less risky approach to 'filing' off sharp edges is to use emery or other abrasive paper that has been glued to a length of wood. This is also less likely to damage the chuck or other parts of the lathe if (or when) it goes where it isn't meant to.

# 10   More Advanced Lathework

## USING A STEADY

Steadies are attachments that support the work being turned with adjustable 'fingers'. These are usually made from plain bronze, which creates the obvious requirement that the surface on which the fingers rub should be both round and smooth. The work slides over the fingers so it is important to ensure they are well lubricated – an excess of neat cutting oil is sufficient. Although fixed and travelling steadies appear quite similar, their uses are rather different.

## Fixed Steady

The fixed steady is used to support long work held in a chuck (Fig. 10.1). The steady needs to be threaded over the work. Ideally, the work will have a constant outer diameter that allows the steady to be moved up close to the chuck and secured temporarily to the bed (with its locking nut). The fingers can now be adjusted individually to run on the outer diameter of the work, supporting it without shake but not binding on it (Fig. 10.2). The steady should now be slid along the bed and reclamped in a position that allows the necessary machining operations such as facing, boring or turning to be carried out.

If it is not possible to set the steady in this way, an alternative is to centre-drill the work and then support its far end temporarily with a centre (or a tailstock chuck if the work is small enough). With luck, this will allow the work to be held accurately enough for

Fig. 10.1 The fixed steady is used to support long work that cannot be supported by a centre.

Fig. 10.2 Moving the steady close to the chuck allows the support fingers to be set accurately.

the steady to be set. Caution should be taken not to set the steady so it deflects the work – if it does it will cause the work to flex back and forth with each rotation and could potentially cause the work to 'walk' out of the chuck.

## Travelling Steady

A travelling steady or 'follow rest' appears very similar to a fixed steady, except it attaches to the saddle so it is in a fixed position relative to the tool and it has two, rather than three fingers. The fingers are placed to oppose the forces created by the cutting tool that pushes the work backwards and upwards. Its function is to support thin workpieces that would otherwise flex away from the chuck and that may or may not be supported at the tailstock end. Note that a travelling steady usually runs on the larger diameter of the work, rather than the reduced part behind the cut.

## TAPER TURNING

In principle, taper turning is easy on any lathe with a compound top slide as all that needs to be done is to turn the slide to the appropriate angle (Fig. 10.3), lock the saddle and use the top slide to take the cuts. Of course, nothing is that simple, with the real difficulty being adjusting the top slide to exactly the right angle. Mini-lathes typically have a graduated scale reading 45 degrees either side of square attached to the top slide (Fig.10.4). Unfortunately, these are rarely more accurate than about a degree and although they are fine for setting up 'ornamental tapers', they are not good enough for tapers that need to match an existing part. It is possible to turn accurate tapers and the best way to explain this is to detail the making of a taper to fit the lathe's number 2 Morse tailstock.

*Fig. 10.3 The top slide needs to be retracted to allow it to be set at an angle.*

*Fig. 10.4 The degree scale should only be relied upon for approximate angle setting.*

## Turning a Morse Taper

Morse tapers, along with Brown and Sharpe, Jacobs, Jarno and a few others, are one of several series of standard fittings that fall into the class of 'self holding tapers'. With an included angle of only a few degrees, the 'wedging' action of such tapers means it is possible to twist two components together gently to get a firm, and accurately concentric, fit. This combination of simplicity and accuracy means such tapers are almost universal on lathes and milling machines. Mini-lathes have an MT3 taper in the headstock and an MT2 taper in the tailstock. The allowable error in the taper is just 0.002in per foot, in the direction that increases the taper. On an MT3 taper, that is just half-a-thou error in diameter.

Many tools and accessories mount in either the mandrel or the tailstock and all need a Morse taper fitting. Making these tapers demands some precision so why should you do it? While it is possible to buy 'blank arbors', turning your own is an excellent way to understand your lathe's capabilities.

Turning a taper is, in theory, achieved easily. The top slide (compound rest) is set at a suitable angle and cuts are taken solely by moving the top slide by hand. It is getting the angle correct that is the challenge. Assuming the tailstock is set up accurately, the classic way of doing this is shown in the photographs. The work is centre-drilled and a fixed centre clamped between the work and another centre in the tailstock. A dial indicator is fitted to the toolpost, with its tip on the centreline of the taper, and is moved back and forth (Fig. 10.5). The angle of the slide is adjusted until there is no movement in the needle along the whole length of the taper.

There are a few flaws with this method. You need a few tools that you may not have: two centres and a tailstock drill. Moreover, even a small error in the alignment of the tailstock makes the exercise pointless.

If you do not have the equipment to set up the work in this way, start with a sharp tool at centre height and set the top slide at an angle of about 2 degrees. There is no point in using a roughing out tool, as you will only be taking light cuts (Fig. 10.6). Use the dial on the slide as a guide but be aware this only gives an approximation. To turn a satisfactory taper, you will need almost all the full travel of the top slide. Make sure the gib strips for the slides are adjusted with no shake and wind the slide back as far as is possible without any looseness becoming apparent. Move the cross slide and set the tool at the end of the workpiece.

All cuts are taken with the top slide, advancing the cross slide initially by 0.010in for each cut. Note how rapidly the taper advances along the work with each cut. As soon as the taper will enter an MT2 socket, it should be tested. An MT2-3 adaptor sleeve makes this easy (Fig. 10.7) but if you do not have one you can use the tailstock. This has the disadvantage that you cannot 'wobble' the tailstock to check for a good fit. To check the taper, use a thin smear of engineer's blue (the non-setting 'microm-eter paste', not marking out blue) although a line drawn with a fat magic marker is just as good. Push the taper home, then rotate the chuck and taper gently by hand. If the line is smeared along its length, well done! More likely, it will only be smeared or rubbed off at one end. Loosen off the top slide, adjust the taper gently by a fraction and take a cut – just a few thou this time – and re-test. A dial indicator can be used to measure these small adjustments in angle and make life a little easier. Eventually, you will find the mark is being rubbed off evenly along its whole length. You will also find, at this point, the taper will fit much more firmly and easily in the socket. The sudden change is usually quite obvious and there should be no wobble at all.

It is now a case of taking sufficient further cuts to ensure the whole length of the taper enters the socket. The final cut should be

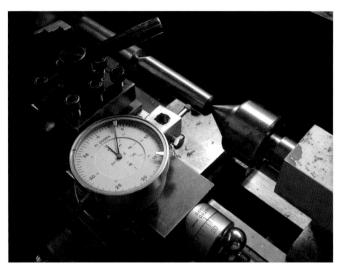

*Fig. 10.5 Angling the top slide to copy a Morse taper.*

*Fig. 10.6 Turning a taper using an angled top slide.*

*Fig. 10.7 Testing an MT2 taper with an MT2-MT3 adapter sleeve.*

shallow. If using an HSS tool, make sure it is sharp with a small flat or a radius on its tip to get a good finish. To further improve the finish quality, turn the slide handle by twisting both ends of the handle, rather than just one, as steadily as you can without pausing. Traversing the tool backwards 'crossing the thread' of the original cut can bring a final improvement. Using a slow electric screwdriver with a section of 5mm Allen key to turn the handle is a useful tip for getting a really smooth finish.

If you really struggle to get a good taper, here are two tips. Rough turn an over-length blank and then turn two narrow raised strips to exact size at each end of the taper. Once these are a perfect fit, they can be machined away to create a full-length taper at the correct setting. Another idea is to 'waist' a taper by machining away the central section. This will be particularly useful if you struggle to get your cutters on centre height as any vertical error will slightly belly the taper. From time to time, you may encounter high quality tools with their shanks relieved in this way.

Once you have a perfect taper, don't move the cross slide! I suggest you turn three or more tapers, and you will probably wish you had done more (Fig. 10.8). It is worth noting that, although in theory it is possible to produce MT3 tapers to fit the headstock mandrel in this way, there is a problem. The top slide simply doesn't have the travel to cut a full length MT3 taper in

*Fig. 10.8 Once you have the setting right, it's worth making a small stock of taper arbors.*

*Fig. 10.9 This 'curve' is two tapers and a straight section blended together.*

one cut, although with care the cut can be made in two stages. Nonetheless, short or 'stub form' tapers are adequate for many uses and you may well decide this will be adequate for any job you have in hand. Stub tapers should be made to fit the large end of the socket.

## Other Tapers

To cut other tapers, internal or external, to match an existing part, you can simply follow the above procedure. It's also possible to create decorative curves by 'blending' different tapers together with emery cloth glued to a backing board (Fig. 10.9). It pays to have an engineer's protractor as this can be used to make a reasonably accurate measurement of the matching part and to set the starting angle for the compound slide.

Sometimes it is useful to make a simple jig square to assist with resetting the top slide for some tapers that you may need to use over and again. One example is the 8 degree angle used for ER-series collets, where a simple 8 degree 'square' can be used to assist making both collet holders and custom collets (Fig. 10.10).

## Offsetting the Tailstock

For tapers that are too long to be cut by angling the tailstock, an alternative

*Fig. 10.10 An 8 degree square made for setting the top slide to match ER collets.*

approach is to offset the tailstock. Usually this is done with the work mounted between centres. Clearly, when the centres are offset in this way the work is not supported very rigidly so cuts have to be light.

Occasionally the flexibility of long, thin work can be an advantage, for example where one end of a very thin valve rod is held in a three-jaw chuck and the other end is slightly offset. Be aware this approach will produce an elegantly curved taper, not a straight one.

## Taper Turning Attachments

Although no taper turning attachments are currently marketed for mini-lathes, a web search will turn up a number of examples, and a very well thought out example by Michael Cox was published in *Model Engineers' Workshop*.

## Making Matching Custom Tapers

If you simply want to cut your own tapers to fit each other, then the exact angle is not important. However, setting with an engineer's protractor may still be worth doing as this helps ensure the resulting taper is of an appropriate length. Ideally, you should cut internal and external tapers at the same setting. Clearly, this involves some creative working as if you want to cut an internal taper starting at the large end, you will need to support the matching external taper at the small end. As always, there are ways around this. One is to cut the internal taper by 'poking' the tool through the small end of the work. This can work well for a flywheel or similar fairly thin part, which can made first, removed and used as a gauge to test the matching external taper.

This approach is no good for a socket in the end of a shaft but the reversible drive of mini-lathes comes to the rescue as, if the internal taper is turned conventionally, the matching external taper can be made with the tool at the back of the work and the lathe turning in reverse.

## Taper Reamers

Another idea that is particularly useful if you want to make a number of small interchangeable tapers and matching sockets is to make your own taper reamer at the same time as making a stock of taper blanks (Fig. 10.11). The reamer itself can be turned from silver steel, ground away to half its diameter like a D-bit, and hardened and tempered.

## FORM TOOLS

Tapers are far from the only 'special' shape you may need to turn. Form tools are those with the cutting edge shaped to create a special profile in the work. The simplest form tools could be square ended like a parting tool to create square grooves, with a circular tip for round grooves or rounded fillets

Fig. 10.11 A tapered D-bit and some stub tapers turned at the same setting to match a light indexing attachment.

Fig. 10.12 This form tool from gauge plate can be used to make spheres.

such as those at the root of a railway tyre. Hollow-ended form tools can create spheres or rounded ridges (Fig. 10.12). Screwcutting tools are also a type of form tool.

For more demanding shapes, such as those used in making handrail knobs, we can make our own form tools quite simply either by grinding a 'negative' of the required shape into an HSS blank or by making a special tool from gauge plate. Gauge plate is an oil-hardenable steel that (aside from using oil instead of water) can be hardened and tempered in a similar way to silver steel. You should be able to get detailed instructions for this from the supplier of your gauge plate as it can vary depending on the nature of the material supplied.

Taking the example of a handrail knob, this is a very simple tool to make. A hole the same size as the head of the knob can be drilled at a slight angle (to provide some front clearance), then half of it is filed away and the left side shaped for the stem and boss. After hardening, tempering and a final polish the tool can be mounted with its upper surface at lathe centre height and it is simply fed gently into the work to create the knob. The knobs are finished by turning the straight mounting spigot and parting off, then threading by hand. If the cross holes are drilled before shaping, it becomes very easy to turn out a whole series of knobs, all the same (Fig. 10.13).

Although there is a limit to how large such form tools can be, especially for use on steel, it is surprising how large an item can be formed in brass. A mini-lathe is quite capable of making 10mm (⅜in) balls in brass (Fig. 10.14).

Form tools may also be used to make gear cutters using the 'button' method but more detail on gear cutting is beyond the scope of this book (Fig. 10.15).

Fig. 10.13 Using a form tool makes it easy to produce large numbers of matching parts.

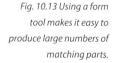

*Fig. 10.14 This brass knob was made using a form tool.*

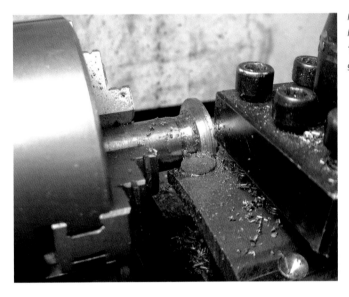

*Fig. 10.15 Using a hardened silver-steel 'button' to make a gear cutter.*

*Fig. 10.16 Making a pulley for a poly-V belt with a V-form tool.*

Another use of form tools is to create pulley grooves, such as those used for poly V-belts. This is a relatively simple exercise as, if the tool is ground to the correct angle cutting the grooves is merely a matter of feeding the tool in at the correct spacing and depth for the belt used (Fig. 10.16).

Thread cutting is another example of using a form tool but due to the complexities of the process, this process has a chapter of its own.

## BORING BETWEEN CENTRES

A variation on normal boring makes use of a 'between centres boring bar'. This is a long shaft that fits literally between two late centre and is driven by a 'dog', with an adjustable cutter somewhere near the middle of its length. In use, a large workpiece is attached to the cross slide of the lathe (this is easier to do on lathes with a T-slotted table) or a vertical slide set crosswise. The work must have a hole large enough for the bar to be threaded through and is adjusted so the boring bar is right on the centre line of the desired hole. The cut is taken by moving the work from one side of the cutter to the other and put on by making adjustments to the cutter's protrusion from the bar.

This is an accurate process but a long, slow one to set up (Fig. 10.17). However, it is worth knowing about as it may be the only way to bore a hole in a really large or awkward casting. For relatively short holes or, for example, to take a 'segment' out of a thick plate, it may be possible to hold a long boring tool in a four-jaw chuck instead of using a between centres bar (Fig. 10.18). It may also be feasible to clamp such workpieces to the toolpost. It is possible to make a T-slotted cross slide to replace the standard cross slide for those who want to maximize the capabilities of their machine (Fig. 10.19).

## PARTING LARGER DIAMETERS

In the previous chapter we practised parting off relatively small diameter stock. It is possible to part off steel 50mm (2in) in diameter on a mini-lathe in the way described (Fig. 10.20) but some people simply cannot succeed in parting off larger diameters conventionally. If this is your experience there are two options worth considering. The first is a 'pedestal' type tool that has a tall, narrow support lodged between the blade and the top of the cross slide. There are various designs and, although I have heard positive comments about them, I don't have direct experience of this type of tool.

Many small lathe users advocate a second approach – a rear toolpost with an inverted parting tool fitted to it. This was a normal arrangement on many manual production lathes as it allowed turning followed by parting without a tool change, which was popular with machinists on piece work. It does also seem to be less liable to chatter and digging in. Explanations range from different forces on the saddle, through the tool tending to spring out instead of in, to the simple idea the swarf can fall out of the cut.

In principle, a rear toolpost, with a central fixing bolt, could easily be made to fit above a tapped hole at the rear of a mini-lathe cross slide. A simpler idea is to mount a parting tool upside down in the normal toolpost and run the lathe in reverse, although there is a risk this could lift the saddle off the inverted V and make matters worse.

It's up to you to decide but, with a well-adjusted machine and a bit of confidence, you may discover more complex solutions are unnecessary.

A 1940s article by 'LBSC', who wrote profusely in *Model Engineer* over many decades, advocated a useful tool, not for parting off but for the similar task of making deep, wide grooves in large diameters. The tool has the shape of a fish's tail in plan view. In use, it is fed in five to ten thou at one side of the groove, moved across to the other side of

Fig. 10.17 Setting up a casting on the cross slide ready for boring.

Fig. 10.18 This stout boring bar is held in the chuck, rather than between centres, but is still being used to bore a casting fixed to the cross slide.

Fig. 10.19 A T-slotted cross slide is a useful modification for boring between centres.

*Fig. 10.20 It is possible – parting off a ring more than 2in in diameter.*

the groove and fed in again before the return journey. Another respected writer, Tubal Cain, advised a similar tool for turning crankshaft bearings.

When you first attempt parting of larger diameters you will encounter 'dig-ins' and 'chatter'. In time, you can overcome these by following the earlier advice – and discover the huge difference made by running a brush full of neat cutting oil in the groove. Most of all, have the confidence to feed in and get a positive cut. A well set up mini-lathe with a good tool should reliably part off mild steel at least 38mm (1½in) in diameter or more (Fig. 10.21).

Notwithstanding the above, you might

find yourself in the position of a minority of mini-lathe owners, who, having tried every tip and wrinkle, still cannot part off larger diameters successfully. This may mean you have one of the 'unlucky' machines fitted with an unusually loose grade of ball bearings. The standard (ball raced) bearings fitted to mini-lathes are pretty hefty units and able to take a considerable load but, depending on the source of the bearings on any particular unit (particularly some of the cheaper 'brands'), you may get ones made to lower specifications. Certainly, a proportion of mini-lathe owners report persistent problems with surface finish, chatter and particularly with parting off,

*Fig. 10.21 A ring and disc parted off in a mini-lathe. The coils of swarf show how well the tool was cutting.*

although in recent years there have been fewer such complaints. If you have tried every other avenue to eliminate problems when parting off, refer to the section on fitting angular contact or roller bearings. It is quite a big task but worthwhile and surprisingly cost effective. If this is the case, you may find replacing the mandrel bearings in the headstock with roller bearings is useful. *See* Chapter 14 on accessories and upgrades.

## INTERNAL GROOVES

Some boring bars allow the tool to be fitted in such a way as to facilitate cutting internal grooves, as might be needed for a 'banjo' fitting, eccentric strap or an internal O-ring, for example. Figure 10.22 shows a selection of 3.2mm (⅛in) HSS bits made to be held in a boring bar and used to cut internal grooves and threads.

It can be difficult to zero the tool with confidence under these circumstances, and the best technique is to use your ears while turning the lathe slowly by hand. Bear in mind internal grooving implies a broad cut, rather like parting off, and with the greater spring of a boring tool, chatter is an ever present risk. In many cases, a relatively poor finish won't be a problem but using sharp tools, gentle feed and modest speeds will help minimize problems.

## KNURLING

Knurling is rather different from all the techniques we have looked at so far because it produces a pattern that may be both decorative and functional but does not have to have any great level of precision.

Knurls are produced by a process that is a combination of both cutting and forming, so the finished knurl will be slightly greater in diameter than the starting stock. The basic knurling technique is to force one or two hardened metal wheels with sharp-edged raised ridges into the work. If the

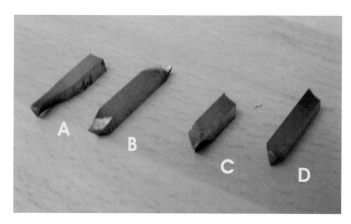

Fig. 10.22 Toolbits from 3.2mm (⅛in) HSS for internally threading, grooving and shaping an ER collet nut.

Despite the apparent simplicity of the knurling process, many beginners have difficulties in getting a good crisp knurl, with a particular problem being the generation of a very fine pattern with twice the pitch intended. Some authors have complex routes to calculating the exact diameter for a perfect knurl but, in fact, the best way is simply to make sure the knurls are applied quite rapidly and forcefully at first. This is easiest if knurling is started on one edge of the work. With about a quarter to a third of the knurl riding gently on the surface of the work, apply a good dose of cutting fluid and then feed the knurls rapidly in until they bite (Fig. 10.25). Now feed the knurls gently back and forth across the full width of the area

Fig. 10.23 A robustly built scissors knurling device for mini-lathes.

possible to use simple knurls on a mini-lathe, even up to a diameter of 65mm (2½in), which is beyond the capacity of most scissor knurls (Fig. 10.24).

Fig. 10.24 The large diameter on this dial was knurled with a single wheel mounted on a bar in the mini-lathe toolpost.

wheel(s) have a straight pattern then they will produce a straight knurl on the work but many knurls come as a pair with diagonal ridges angled in opposite directions. These diagonal knurls will produce a diamond pattern on the work. Both types of knurl are available in fine, medium and coarse sizes, the difference being the size of the pattern.

There are various types of knurling tool. The two that are most likely to be encountered are the simple types that rely on the knurl being pushed into the work and the 'scissors' type where the two wheels are opposed above and below the work and closed on it using a screw. For mini-lathes, the scissors knurl is often recommended as this has balanced forces and does not strain the machine (Fig. 10.23). It is, however,

Fig. 10.25 A small scissors knurl with a capacity of about 25mm (1in).

to be treated. Use an oily brush to keep the pattern clear of swarf and lubricated, and increase the feed until the knurls start to show nice crisp edges or points at the top of the pattern.

Usually, the knurled area will have areas of a smaller diameter at each side. If you leave the knurled diameter over width then any distortion of the pattern at the edges can be turned off afterwards to ensure a good clean pattern across the full final width.

## TURNING COMPLEX SHAPES

From time to time you may need to generate relatively complex shapes or curves. For spheres or circular curves then a special rotating tool-holder called a radius-turning attachment can be used. There is one available for mini-lathes that is suitable for turning balls and convex surfaces (Fig. 10.26). The attachment replaces the cross slide and has an 'up and over' action that requires a degree of care.

For other shapes it is possible to use a technique called 'co-ordinate working'. Simply draw out the curve you need on

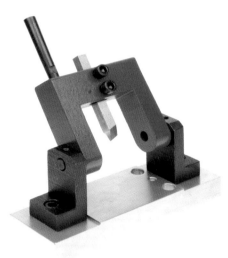

Fig. 10.26 A mini-lathe ball turning tool that fits to the cross slide.

graph paper (or in a CAD program on your computer) and calculate the infeed required at a series of points along the length of the work. With patience and care, you can produce the shape you need gradually either using a series of facing cuts, each to the depth indicated by your diagram, or normal turning cuts of different lengths at increasing depth. The process is made

easier by keeping the steps all the same size, say 0.5mm, a half-turn of the top slide handle, and having all the depths listed on a sheet of paper so you can cross them off one by one.

Naturally, the finished result will have a series of small steps in it (these can be minimized by using a round-nosed tool) that need to be removed carefully but the final result can be very pleasing (Fig. 10.27).

Fig. 10.27 A complex curve turned using the co-ordinate method.

# 11   Making Holes

The boring of holes has been covered in detail in earlier chapters. There are many other ways of making holes using a lathe. We have touched on drilling holes; a drill or similar tool can be held in a chuck in the spindle and used to drill work attached to the toolpost or a vertical slide, or braced against a 'drill pad' in the tailstock (Fig. 11.1). Similarly, other types of hole-making tools, including reamers or a boring head, can be used in this way. A drilling spindle (either a specialist item or improvised, such as a rotary tool) can be mounted on the toolpost and used to drill stationary work in various directions, including along and across the axis of the lathe. Typically, we want to make holes in a part already attached to the spindle, probably because it needs to be concentric with round surfaces we have already turned. When accuracy of boring is not needed or practical this is normally done using a tailstock chuck, in combination with various types of hole-making tools. Essentially one is operating the machine like a drilling machine in reverse, with the work rotating.

## TWIST DRILLS

Most readers will be familiar with ordinary twist drills, typically used as general purpose drills for much DIY. These are readily available in sets at $\frac{1}{32}$ or $\frac{1}{64}$in and 0.5mm intervals, although the range of quality available varies hugely. Price is a fair, but not absolute, indicator of quality, although do avoid the very cheapest sets as they will only cause frustration. You can pay a premium for various types of coating but, aside from

being made of a good grade of steel, the most important feature is how well a drill is sharpened. New drills should have a pair of straight, sharp cutting edges that are well matched for length.

You may already have one or two sets like this but will soon find yourself wanting other 'odd' sizes. A good way to start is by obtaining a mid-priced set of either metric drills in 0.1mm steps, ideally up to 13mm (Fig. 11.2). If you prefer imperial sizes, you should be able to find a boxed set combined with a full set of number and letter drills. Either solution will provide you with all the sizes you need for 99 per cent of drilling operations. Assuming you haven't paid an arm and a leg for these drills, from time to time you will break or damage one or find one that won't sharpen well. Naturally, these will tend to be in the sizes you use most and this is when it's worth paying a bit extra to replace them with high-quality drill bits. This way you will never be short of sizes but your stock of drills will increase gradually in quality and reliability, with the new bits targeting your most used sizes.

*Fig. 11.1 This 'drill pad' can be used to support work mounted in the tailstock.*

*Fig. 11.2 About to use a 13mm drill on cast iron. The hole has already been opened up to 11mm.*

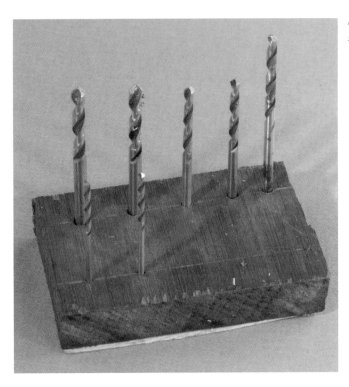

*Fig. 11.3 A selection of spotting drills.*

standard drills will often wander rather than bite straight into a flat metal surface. It also increases the pressure required to penetrate the metal. Any standard drill expected to make an accurate hole should be started in an accurate centre created with a spotting drill or a centre drill. When drilling holes wider than about 3mm (⅛in) it always pays to do so in more than one stage ('step drilling'), with the last but one drill being only a little smaller than the final drill size.

Two other drill point geometries have been devised to overcome this limitation of the standard drill point. The 'split point' geometry is like a standard point but has secondary relief ground behind the main cutting edge, reducing the size of the drill 'point' greatly. The 'four facet' geometry uses a straight cutting edge with straight relief, and sometimes even a third pair of facets. Both split point and four-facet drills are much more accurate and need less pressure in use but they also cost more.

## Drill Geometry

The most common types of drill you will find have a point angle of 118 degrees and this is accepted as the best 'general purpose' angle. Sometimes you may find drills with relatively blunt tips. These are used for cutting sheet metal as they are less likely to 'grab' the metal as they break through.

Drills come in various length. Standard drills are known as 'jobber's drills' and shorter ones as 'stub drills'. Look out for short spotting drills with 90 degree points (Fig. 11.3). These are good as centring drills (not 'centre drills') and it's useful to have a few in different sizes as they tend not to wander and are used to mark the point where a larger drill will be used to make a hole. They seem to last longer than 'centre drills' and work just as well.

You can also find 'long series' drills, which are, unsurprisingly, used for drilling long, deep holes. However, be aware they have a greatly increased tendency to wander from a straight line.

Other variations include 'slow' and 'fast' spirals. Slow spiral and straight flute drills are good for brasses, bronzes and sheet metals as they have less tendency to grab the work. Fast spiral drills are used for plastics as they generate less heat and holes 'melted' into plastic are rarely accurate!

Finally, as far as metal drills are concerned, there are three types of drill point you will encounter (Fig. 11.4). The standard tip has two coned surfaces but the shortcoming of this design is that a short, straight edge is left across the centre of the drill. This is why

*Fig. 11.4 Three types of drill point – the usual cone type, split point and four facet.*

## Sharpening Twist Drills

This book is not the place for a long treatise on drill sharpening but it is worth considering how you intend to keep your drills sharp. Blunt drills cut oversize, ill-aligned holes, produce a poor finish and are generally frustrating to use. A good drill can be resharpened dozens of times and may have a life of several decades!

It is possible to grind standard and four-facet drill types offhand on a bench grinder, although there is a considerable 'knack' to achieving accurate, equal edges with the correct relief. Although some users profess to be able to equal the results of any jig, few mortals can achieve such results, although a hand-sharpened drill may well be better than a blunt one! Alternatively, there are various attachments that profess to offer perfect twist drills every time. These are either used with a standard bench grinder or use one of many types of jig with a built-in grinding stone. Success with these seems to depend on a combination of luck, practice and personal preference as much as the innate qualities of any device. When buying one, compare the price with how much it would cost to replace drills every time one breaks or gets blunt, let alone the inconvenience of waiting for an odd size to come in the post.

## DRILL CHUCKS

Twist drills can be held in a three-jaw, or even a four-jaw, chuck to drill work held on the cross slide by any reasonable means. If you do this often, then a large 13mm capacity chuck on an MT3 arbor may be useful to you or alternatively get a 2–3MT adaptor for a tailstock chuck. You are more likely to want to use a drill chuck in the tailstock. You may be able to obtain a drill and MT2 arbor as a package or have to order them separately. If you do, remember not only to specify the MT2 taper for the tailstock but a matching fitting for the drill chuck. Cheap drill chucks often have a threaded fitting and better quality ones will use one of several different taper standards. All that really matters is that chuck and arbor match each other.

You may find yourself with the choice of a tanged arbor or one threaded for a drawbar. Neither is ideal for the mini-lathe tailstock as a tanged arbor won't let you fully retract the tailstock without ejecting the chuck and a drawbar arbor may fail to eject properly, and you can't use it with a drawbar anyway. The majority of mini-lathe users choose tanged arbors but cut off the tang by using an abrasive wheel in a rotary tool. It ain't pretty but it works.

Another choice is between keyed and keyless chucks. Keyed chucks require you to keep track of the tightening key and, surprisingly, are often harder to tighten than keyless chucks (Fig. 11.5). Good quality keyless chucks are quite costly but excellent to use (Fig. 11.6), while cheap (typically plastic bodied) keyless chucks are best avoided. In contrast, even fairly inexpensive

*Fig. 11.5 A very nice small keyed Jacobs chuck on an MT2 arbor.*

*Fig. 11.6 Keyless chucks have a phenomenal grip.*

*Fig. 11.7 This tiny chuck on an MT1 arbor will hold drills down to less than 0.50mm (0.020in). It needs an MT1 to MT2 adapter to be used with a mini-lathe.*

keyed chucks are usually usable and are a good choice if funds are tight. Be aware that keyless chucks are self-tightening so it's worth having some sort of strap wrench handy as well as a tommy bar to assist with undoing one.

You will almost certainly find the need to hold drills up to 13mm (½in) diameter from time to time (although you should not try to drill that wide in one go on the lathe) so make sure you have a chuck capable of taking such drills. It is also worth having one or more smaller chucks, perhaps a very small

0–6mm (0–¼in), for precision work (Fig. 11.7) and a 10mm (⅜in) chuck for general use. It is always worth looking out for drill chucks at boot sales and the like. Jacobs chucks are particularly well made, especially the taper-fitting ones – they do make budget screw-on chucks for hand drills. Try to avoid chucks in poor condition, although if you find you have picked up a stiff or hard to tighten one, it can be used to hold a centre drill or spotting drill semi-permanently. A chuck with a damaged socket, one that is truly inaccurate or bell-mouthed is best left

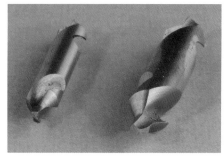

*Fig. 11.8 This small drill chuck piggybacked in a larger one has a hand grip but can rotate freely, allowing the sensitive drilling of tiny holes.*

*Fig. 11.9 A pair of large centre drills.*

alone, although I have one such chuck that just serves as a handle for a deburring bit.

There are a few variations on tailstock drill chucks and one alternative has the chuck mounted like a rotating centre. These are used as steadies to support long, thin work and are really only useful if you do a lot of work on such items. Another arrangement has a small chuck mounted on a sliding, free-turning bar that runs inside an MT2 holder (Fig. 11.8). These can be used with very small drills. Sometimes these have a lever feed arrangement – known as 'sensitive drilling attachments'. For others, the right hand is used to hold a knurled disk behind the chuck to gently prevent it from spinning and to apply cutting pressure. If the drill starts to jam, one simply releases the disk and avoids a broken drill bit. These chucks can also be used, with care, to tap small holes under power, again letting it spin if the tap binds or bottoms out.

It is not always essential to use a drill chuck – it is possible to obtain drills of almost any size with Morse taper shanks. Although they are often rather expensive new, they turn up regularly at car boot sales. I have a few in useful sizes larger than 13mm (½in) and they are particularly useful when preparing a hole for finishing by boring.

## Drilling a Hole

If you want an accurate hole, drilling is not as simple as selecting the right drill, spinning up the work and pushing it in. First of all, fit the drill chuck in the tailstock. Make sure both the arbor and the socket are clean and free from swarf (a tapered bit of softwood is an excellent socket-cleaning tool), and the arbor should fit firmly in place with no more than a push and twist motion.

It always pays to start with an accurate centre hole as this gives the drill the maximum chance of truly following the axial centre line of the work. As you might

*Fig. 11.10 Using a centre drill to put a coned hole in the end of a special fitting.*

expect, centre drills are often used for this (Fig. 11.9), although their true purpose is putting in coned holes (with a central oil reservoir) for between centres turning. They do the job well enough, although expect to break the tip off one every once in a while. It is usually possible to pick the broken end out with the tip of a scriber. Centre drills can also be handy when you need an accurate 60 degree hole for other purposes, such as making pipe unions (Fig. 11.10).

The job is better done using special 'spotting drills', which are short and stiff and are designed to start a hole without wandering. It's well worth getting a few such spotting drills as they are much less fragile than centre drills (picking the broken tip of a centre drill out of the bottom of a hole is a rite of passage for many new lathe owners). They are only used to make a conical depression and start a hole so you don't need a full

set of sizes, just four or five, and always use the largest one that is smaller than the hole you are drilling.

When starting a hole, whether with a centre drill or stub drill, make sure the surface is flat. If facing off has left a centre pip, file it away as it *will* make the drill tip wander off target. Now drill your hole in stages, starting with a rather undersized drill and typically no more than 6mm (¼in in diameter), and then going up in steps according to how comfortable the drills are cutting the material in question. Retract the tailstock barrel and adjust the position of the tailstock so the drill is just outside the hole. This is where a lever locking tail-stock comes into its own. Apply the cut by winding the tailstock handwheel gently and advancing the bit into the metal. Retract the drill regularly (again, much easier with a lever locking tailstock) to clear the drill flutes of swarf. Failure to do this will make the drill bind. The consequences of this will range from a broken drill (in smaller sizes) to the chuck arbor spinning in its socket. Clearly both of these things should be avoided if at all possible.

A typical speed for drilling a 6mm (¼in) hole in mild steel is 1,500 rpm. Clearly, when drilling small holes or soft materials in the lathe it will be difficult to run the drill as fast as it ought to be worked. On the other hand, the lathe is well suited to drilling larger holes, with the variable speed being a great aid to 'keeping the drill happy'. As for how fast to wind the tailstock, I think it's best to judge this by feel rather than any formula. In general, a happy drill will produce good clean swarf from both flutes of the drill and won't make any unpleasant sounds. I always use drills in 'less preferred' sizes for opening up a hole in stages, as it reduces the wear on my 'best' drills. It's worth mentioning you may be surprised how quickly a drill can remove metal compared to a lathe tool. I am not sure why this is the case but I suspect it is because the two flutes of a drill create more balanced cutting forces.

Fig. 11.11 Crude but effective – using insulation tape to help drill a hole to depth.

If the hole is to be left drilled, make the last but one hole rather smaller (by say 0.5-1mm or ¹⁄₃₂-¹⁄₆₄in) than the finished size. This means the last drill will have very little to do and will cut close to its nominal size. If you are finishing the hole by reaming or boring, see under those sections for how much material to leave.

If you need to drill several holes all to the same depth you can use depth stops in the form of small rings that lock on to the drill with a grub screw. For single holes or less critical jobs, a simple piece of insulation tape wrapped around the drill is a quick and easy alternative but do make sure it isn't pushed out of position by swarf (Fig. 11.11).

In industry, for most materials a 'jet' of coolant would be directed into the hole, helping to wash out swarf and cool the drill. I never use a full flood of coolant but I do use a brush to ensure the drill remains 'wet' with neat cutting oil. This reduces the drill-ing pressure greatly but can cause swarf to stick in the flutes of the drill, so remember to withdraw the drill regularly, and at any indi-cation of binding, and clean the flutes with an oily brush.

## STEP DRILLS AND CONE DRILLS

Despite their name, step drills are not used to drill deep holes in multiple passes. They are normally used for opening up large holes in sheet material but can be useful where accurately sized holes are needed in material not more than about 5mm (³⁄₁₆in) thick (Fig. 11.12).

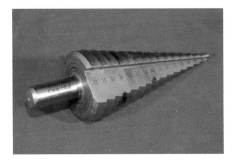

Fig. 11.12 Step drills are usually used for sheet materials but can be handy for making accurate holes in any thin material.

Similarly, cone drills are intended for drilling sheet material but can be of use for putting a gently chamfered lead on holes, useful when you need to guide something such as a piston into a bore.

## DRILLING FROM THE HEADSTOCK

Occasionally, you may need to drill from the headstock, such as opening up work attached to the cross slide ready for boring or drilling work supported on the toolpost or on a 'drilling pad' inserted in the tailstock. In principle, there are no special steps that need to be taken, aside from ensuring the work is held securely so it cannot spin.

## REAMING

While drilling will give reasonably round accurate holes, they are rarely accurate enough for purposes such as bearings or for locating parts together accurately. Boring will give us very round, accurate holes but there is a 'third way' that allows the rapid, repeatable production of accurate holes – reaming.

A reamer is simply a specialized form of drill, with many more flutes, typically six to eight (Fig. 11.13). They are designed to take relatively light cuts in the region of 0.10–0.25mm (0.004–0.010in), while the flutes stabilize the cutting action to give an accurately sized, well-finished hole. The 'H6' reamers that are normally sold as 'general purpose reamers' finish a hole that is a close sliding fit for material dead to the nominal size, although reamers that give a variety of other fits are available.

There are two types of reamer with the self-explanatory names of hand and machine reamers.

*Fig. 11.14 Using a 'hand reamer' in a tailstock chuck to finish the bore of a flywheel.*

### Machine Reamers

The distinguishing feature of machine reamers is they are a constant diameter along their length and, although the flutes are sharpened, they cut on the end. Machine reamers typically have Morse taper shanks so they can be fitted directly in the tailstock of a lathe, with a suitable adapter sleeve if necessary. Machine reamers should be run at about a quarter to half the speed used for a drill of the same size.

### Hand Reamers

A tapered section about 25mm (1in) long at the tip of hand reamers assists with guiding them accurately into a pre-drilled hole. They usually have parallel shanks, with a square

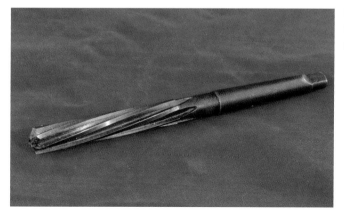

*Fig. 11.13 A machine reamer with spiral flutes and an MT1 shank.*

end to allow fitting a suitable wrench as a handle. The cutting action is different as it takes place on the tapered section, rather than the extreme end. Despite the name, I have not experienced any problems using them in the lathe, held in an ordinary drill chuck and running them a little slower than a machine reamer (Fig. 11.14). The problem with them is if you can only get the end of the hand reamer into the hole, it will end up tapered. From time to time this can prove to be an advantage, such as if you want to make a wheel a force-fit on a shaft.

There is a myth that reamers should take only the lightest 'scrape' from a hole. This is false and manufacturers of reamers and experienced machinists will advise it is important the tool is 'given some work to do' to get the best results. If less than about 0.05mm (0.002in) is left to remove the flutes can deflect instead of cut, causing wear and poor finish.

### Taper Reamers

Taper reamers are available in a wide range of sizes (Fig. 11.15). The larger ones can be used to make taper sockets. Morse taper ones are readily available and are typically available for 'roughing' with notched flutes and 'finishing' with plain flutes or a single

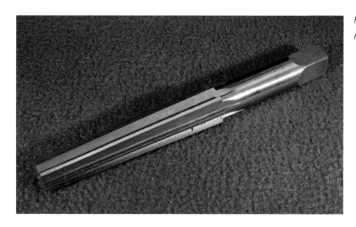

*Fig. 11.15 An MT2 taper reamer.*

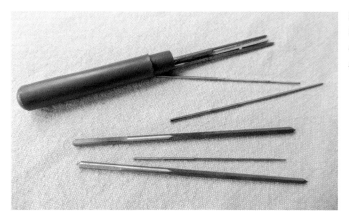

*Fig. 11.16 A set of broaches, used for opening up very small holes.*

*Fig. 11.17 Using a D-bit to form an accurately sized hole in a gearwheel.*

rapidly spiralling flute. Although their usual applications are making new sockets, a Morse taper finishing reamer can be used to salvage a badly scored socket.

Smaller taper reamers are usually intended for making holes for use with taper pins. These are short metal pins in brass or steel used across a diameter to lock wheels or other parts in a fixed relationship with a shaft. Metric taper pins and reamers have a 1:50 taper, while imperial ones have a 1:48 taper – close but not the same.

Except for very short taper pin fittings, it is normal to 'step drill' the hole to leave as little material for the reamer to remove as possible. This is an occasion where the greater control achievable in the lathe compared with a drill press can be a real advantage.

## Broaches

The line between reamers and broaches can be blurred, especially in small sizes. Fluted broaches are effectively small reamers but some broaches simply have five flat facets with relatively sharp edges (Fig. 11.16). They are used in the same way as reamers, to finish small holes, but can remove only very tiny amounts of metal. Very small, gently tapered broaches can be obtained covering sizes from needle-like to about 6mm. These can be used to open up holes carefully to almost any size and are much used by clockmakers. With care, they can be used in the lathe but be aware the smaller sizes are rather fragile.

## D-BITS

From time to time you may need an accurately sized hole that it is not practical to bore or ream, or you may simply not have a reamer the right size. A D-bit is a simple and cheap alternative that has the advantage it can be used to finish a flat-bottomed hole (Fig. 11.17).

The geometry of a D-bit is very simple. It is made from a circular bar of exactly the size of the hole required (Fig. 11.18). This could be an HSS blank or a piece of silver steel (which could be supplied on size or turned down and polished to suit). It is ground or machined away at the end until just over half its diameter remains, then the face of the tool is relieved at about 10 degrees to create a cutting edge. The cutting edge is normally angled across the tool but if a flat-bottomed hole is needed the edge can be straight across to the centre of the tool, and just angled on the non-cutting side. The

*Fig. 11.18 A D-bit made from silver steel.*

very tip of the cutting edge can be angled slightly for strength and to promote getting a good finish. Naturally a carbon steel (silver steel) tool will need hardening and tempering.

If the tool is left like this it will be the near equal of a commercial reamer, if used gently with plenty of lubricant. The drawback is that care has to be taken not to overheat carbon-steel D-bits through aggressive use. Another hazard is the D-bit can clog if a lot of material is removed. One solution to this is to turn down or grind a narrower 'neck' behind the business end of the reamer but this obviously reduces the guiding effect of the full diameter section of the tool.

You may well notice this geometry is very similar to that of HSS boring bars as supplied for use with boring heads, and in many cases the two can be used interchangeably.

## COUNTERSINKS

Countersinks are steeply tapered cutters that are used to create the recesses for countersunk screws and rivets (Fig. 11.19). They can also be used to deburr holes. Beware of cheap countersinks, even if they claim to be

*Fig. 11.19 An HSS countersink intended for use on metal, not wood.*

HSS, because they are usually intended for use on wood. Look for better quality countersinks with relatively few (say four) cutting edges as these work better on metal. Occasionally, you will encounter 'countersinks' with an angled hole though a conical tip. However, these work best as deburring tools, not countersinks.

# 12  Screwcutting

Screwcutting is one of the basic functions of any fully featured engineering lathe so it's surprising to discover a good proportion of lathe users have never tried it. Even so, when one works on a project, sooner or later either the thread is simply too large for a tap or die, it is an awkward size or a degree of accuracy is required that cannot be achieved by other methods in the home workshop.

On lathes, screwcutting is achieved by gearing the mandrel to the leadscrew (Fig. 12.1). If the gearing is 1:1, the thread cut

will be the same pitch as the leadscrew (although not necessarily the same form or diameter). By varying the ratio of the gears via a gearbox or using a set of change gears, screws of various pitches can be cut easily and accurately. This method of screw production was perfected by Henry Maudsley in 1800. Following Sir Joseph Whitworth's standardization of screw threads, this technique for screwcutting played a critical part in the rise of mass production in the nineteenth century.

If we need to produce threads that will only mesh with others we have made, standardization is not an issue. We can use any convenient pitch for the work in hand. In many cases, however, we will want to use bought-in fixings or mate parts with threads cut using standard taps or dies. In these cases we need to cut threads to standard sizes.

Mini-lathes are available in either metric or imperial leadscrew versions. The set of changewheels (Fig. 12.2) allow the cutting of most of the typically encountered metric series threads with a 1.5mm pitch

leadscrew. Similarly, imperial sizes are cut easily with the 16tpi leadscrew. In each case, the various sizes are simple ratios to the leadscrew and the required changewheels are given on tables on the machine and in the manual (Fig. 12.3).

The tables show how to arrange the various change gears. Fitting and setting up the gear trains is, aside from the gear sizes, essentially the same as described previously for setting up the power feed (Fig. 12.4). The exception is when an idler has to be fitted in the middle of the gear train, as in these circumstances any small gear can be fitted outside the idler and the gear on the leadscrew has to be fitted inside, rather than outside, the collar.

Older mini-lathes have a thread indicator dial fitted to the side of the apron (Fig. 12.5). This rotates when the half nuts are disengaged and stops when the nuts are engaged. The numbers on it can be used to ensure you 'pick up' a part cut thread accurately but this only works for more common metric threads on a metric lathe and

*Fig. 12.1 A screwcutting set-up on a mini-lathe. The first and last gears are the same size and all other gears are idlers so that ratio is 1:1 and the cut thread will be the same pitch as the leadscrew.*

*Fig. 12.2 A set of mini-lathe changewheels. This is a metal 'upgrade' set.*

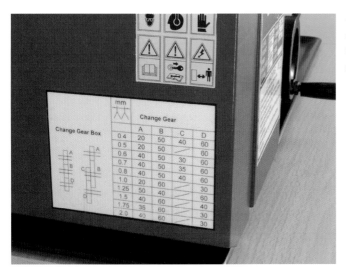

*Fig. 12.3 Most mini-lathes have a thread-cutting table attached to the gearbox cover.*

You will need to fit a suitable threading tool. This could be a bought-in tool or one you have ground yourself from HSS. Like a chamfering tool, it should have top rake running back from the tip and be set with the tip at centre height. For metric threads, this will be a simple 60 degree pointed tool with a slight flat on the end that removes just under a quarter of the thread height. For imperial threads, the tools should have a 55 degree tip and ideally should be rounded off at a radius equal to a third of the thread depth. In practice, just stoning the end of the tool tip will be OK but make sure you do this as a sharp tip will create a point of weakness. Such over-length tools will need to be fed in further than the nominal amount but will not affect the thread materially for most purposes.

You can check the angles of the tool with a screw thread gauge. It should be a good fit for the gauge but if you don't have one you can match the tool against a known good thread, such as a bought-in machine screw.

We will start with the 'simple' approach to screwcutting.

Before cutting the thread, use a centre drill in the tailstock chuck to put a conical hole in the end of the bar. Now extend the bar a few inches and support it with a centre in the tailstock (don't forget a drop of oil in the centre hole if you are using a fixed

*Fig. 12.4 A gear train from the side, showing how the gears overlap.*

If you have a later mini-lathe without a dial and cut odd threads or metric on an imperial lathe (or vice versa) then you will have to leave the leadscrew engaged and use reverse to move the tool back to the start of the thread after each cut.

For a first practice attempt at screwcutting, I suggest you set up a gear train to match the pitch of an existing nut. An M6 nut will have a pitch of 1mm and a ¼in Whitworth nut will be 20tpi, and these are good sizes to start with. Chuck a reasonable length of bar of the right diameter with around 50mm (2in) protruding from the chuck. This will allow you to thread the end while keeping well clear of the chuck jaws.

*Fig. 12.5 The thread dial indicator on an older mini-lathe. These are not fitted to versions with a leadscrew guard.*

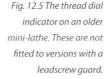

common imperial threads on an imperial lathe. On the lathe or in your manual, you should find a small chart that gives a list of numbers for each thread pitch. By ensuring the index mark is adjacent to one of these numbers, the tool can accurately re-engage with a part cut thread.

centre). This will keep the thread cutting tool well away from the chuck, just in case you are slow in stopping the feed. Thread cutting is also less nerve-racking if you cut a groove for the threading tool to run into. Check the depth of your thread on suitable thread data tables and use a small parting tool to cut a groove slightly deeper than this. You also need to check the tables on the lathe (or in the handbook) to see what index numbers on the thread cutting dial can be used with your chosen thread.

Before using the cutter for the first time, practise using autofeed with the tool backed away from the work. Disengage the clasp nut and put the leadscrew into 'forward' gear at the back of the headstock (this engages the chain of changewheels) (Fig. 12.6). Start the lathe turning slowly and engage the clasp nut by pushing down the lever firmly on the apron as the appropriate number on the thread cutting dial passes the index mark (Fig. 12.7).

Everything will start moving towards the headstock (faster than you expect, if you are only used to the snail-like progress with an auto feed gear-train in place). Keep the lever fully down with gentle pressure, then pull it up and stop the carriage well before anything gets near the chuck! Practise a few times until you are confident you can engage the clasp nuts at the right index number and stop the toolbit in the runout groove cut every time. Note that if you do not hold the lever down it may ride up, spoiling the accuracy of the thread.

Now, make sure the tool is set at centre height and wind the tool in until it just touches the surface. Set the index wheel to zero, then move the toolbit to the right of the work. Take a test cut, just as you did on the practice runs but skimming the surface, stopping the tool in the runout groove and winding it out before returning it to the start (Fig. 12.8).

Assuming the resultant 'spiral scratch' is what you expect, advance the tool by no more than ten divisions (0.25mm or 0.010in)

*Fig. 12.6 Engaging the gear train with the tumbler reverse.*

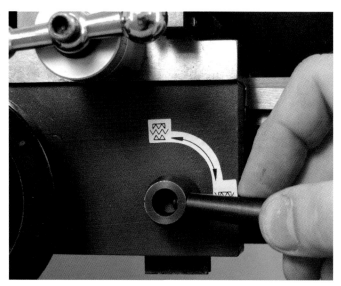

*Fig. 12.7 Engaging the leadscrew clasp nuts.*

*Fig. 12.8 A light skim to check the set-up is correct – note the runout groove.*

and make your first real cut. Make the next cut at about half this depth and gradually reduce to perhaps two divisions (0.05mm or 0.002in) until the thread is at full depth. Disengage the gearbox at the back of the headstock.

To get a proper Whitworth profile you should use a contoured tool called a chaser to round off the top of the threads. A good practical alternative is to use a sponge-backed sanding block to round the top of the threads. Metric threads can be left with a flat top to the threads. Check the fit of the thread in a matching nut before changing any settings, in case you need to take a few more cuts.

### Advanced Thread Cutting Techniques

When cutting relatively small threads similar to the leadscrew in pitch, the approach described above will usually give good results. When the thread depth is significantly larger, the finish of the thread can be improved by angling the top slide to just less than half the thread angle – 29 degrees for a 60 degree metric or unified thread or 27 degrees for a 55 degree imperial thread. If the tool is now advanced using only the top slide, it will do most of its cutting on just the leading face of the tool, halving the cutting forces. The back face of the tool just 'skims' the thread, burnishing it to a good finish.

The problem with this approach is the top slide index dial will not read the depth of cut accurately. This can be solved with a bit of trigonometry but a much easier approach is to move the tooltip forward to touch the work and then zero both the cross slide and top slide indices. Now wind the top slide back so the tool is comfortably clear of the work and advance the cross slide by exactly the required thread depth. You can now put on the cut using the top slide only. When it returns to the zero mark, the thread is at full depth.

Another challenge is cutting either very

*Fig. 12.9 A mandrel handle fitted to an imperial mini-lathe set up to cut a 1mm pitch thread.*

deep or large diameter threads. You may well find the lathe does not have enough torque at the relatively low speeds used for thread cutting to cut a full depth thread under these conditions. The ideal answer is to disconnect the power and use a spindle handle, such as that detailed in the projects section of this book (Fig. 12.9). If you don't have such a handle one alternative is to use a chuck key inserted in each chuck socket in turn as a lever. This makes for very slow progress but if it is the only way to complete an awkward job, it is worth bearing in mind.

The same approach applies to large pitch threads. Do not attempt to screwcut threads coarser than about 3mm pitch or 8tpi directly – the load on the gears with the leadscrew geared up this much is inviting disaster. Such threads can be produced by thread milling using a rotating cutter mounted on the toolpost and driving the mandrel by turning the leadscrew. You will need, however, to make the simple modification of fitting a leadscrew handle.

### INTERNAL THREADS

In principle, cutting internal threads is no different to cutting external ones. In practice, it is much more demanding – not least because you cannot see the tool working inside a hole.

Internal threading tools are essentially like boring bars with suitably shaped tips (Fig. 12.10). It pays to use the stiffest tool you can get that will fit inside the work, although if you are cutting up to an internal shoulder you may need quite a delicately ended tool.

*Fig. 12.10 A very fine-tipped internal threading tool that can work up to shoulder.*

When it comes to actually cutting the thread, it pays to use either a saddle stop or to put a marker on the shank of the tool so you can stop the feed at exactly the same point on each pass. If you use a saddle stop and turn the spindle by hand (for example, with a mandrel handle) then it is possible just to let the threading tool create a single ring groove at the end of the thread, although this does require care.

It pays to cut a circular runout groove inside the work whenever possible as this makes the point where you stop the tool less critical. Indeed, you can listen for the change in sound as the tool stops cutting. The groove can be made with a square-ended bit, like a stubby parting tool, and holding it in a boring bar will suffice.

Take care to ensure the tool is fully clear of the thread before winding it out of the hole and clean out any swarf from inside the hole before each run with the threading tool. As well as risking jamming the tool, any swarf that gets carried up into the cutting area could spoil the thread.

It is not very easy to get a nice shape to the top of an internal thread unless you use specially profiled carbide tips. The best solution is to cut the hole slightly oversize and settle for a truncated thread form. If you do not do this, you will probably end up cutting the thread deeper than it needs to be and making it weaker than if it was slightly truncated.

## UNIVERSAL THREAD CUTTING

What if you wish to cut metric threads on an imperial machine or vice versa? One can change over the leadscrew but this takes time as the apron must be removed and the clasp nuts replaced and adjusted. But there is an easier way

One inch equals precisely 25.4 millimetres. If you combined 100 and 254 tooth changewheel ratios in our set-up, we could convert precisely between the two systems. There is a problem though: a 1-module 254-tooth gear is 256mm (10in) in diameter! A 127-tooth gear could be used, as it is exactly half of 254, but it would still be about 129mm (5in) across. You could accommodate such a gear by making a new mounting banjo but you would also need to add further idler gears. The whole set-up would be rather clumsy.

The answer is a 63-tooth gear (Fig. 12.11). It may seem that 63 is 'close enough' to half of 127 to do the job but it isn't. It would produce errors of around 2 per cent, acceptable for some purposes but not for most. The 63-tooth gear arises from another, fortuitous bit of maths.

A 1mm pitch is 25.4 threads per inch. To cut 25.4tpi on a 16tpi leadscrew you need a

*Fig. 12.11 The aluminium change gear at the back will allow a mini-lathe to translate from imperial to metric threads or vice versa.*

ratio of 16:25.4. This works out at 0.62992:1, or almost exactly 63:100. If you introduce the ratio 63:100 into the gear train then a 16tpi leadscrew will cut a 1mm pitch thread well within the tolerance of any other aspect of the process. To translate this into standard change wheels you can use:

$$63/100 = 63/50 \times \tfrac{1}{2} = 63/50 \times 30/60$$

Conversely, a ratio of 100:63 will allow a 1.5mm pitch metric leadscrew to cut a 16tpi thread with the same accuracy. In fact, the standard metric leadscrew for mini-lathes has a pitch of 1.5mm, which would therefore cut 16 × 1.5 = 24tpi, but this is dealt with by putting the ratios 2/3 and 100:63 in series. To get standard changewheels:

$$100/63 \times 2/3 = 50/63 \times 4/3 = 50/63 \times 4/3$$
$$= 50/63 \times 40/30$$

From these basic ratios, it is possible to derive a ratio for any other metric or imperial thread. Armed with a 63-tooth wheel and the right changewheel ratios you can cut almost any standard thread. It is possible to cut your own 63-tooth wheel but they can also be sourced from hobby suppliers Arc Euro Trade.

Tables showing suggested combinations of changewheels for the three common thread families for both metric and imperial

leadscrews can be downloaded from www.stubmandrel.co.uk – search 'thread cutting'. The tables only use the changewheels supplied with the lathe, plus a 63-tooth gear.

Even with a 63-tooth gear, not all conversions can be absolutely precise, especially for the British Association series. Even so, in the worst cases the ratios given still allow the cutting of threads that will mate with standard threads. In a few cases, better results could be achieved by doubling up gears not duplicated in the standard gear set.

The metric tables cover every preferred value from 0.2mm up to 6mm pitch. The 63-tooth gear allows the imperial machine to produce every thread with no error greater than 0.8 per cent. The imperial table covers all standard BSW, BSF, BSP, UNF, UNC and *Model Engineer* pitches. With the 63-tooth gear, the metric machine can produce all these threads up to 4tpi to better than 0.1 per cent, and up to 2.5tpi with less than a 1 per cent error. The 63-tooth gear also allows both metric and imperial machines to produce all BA threads from 0BA to 16BA, accurate to better than 1 per cent.

Be aware that, when using a conversion gear, you cannot rely on the thread dial indicator to pick up the threads and you will have to modify your working technique to keep the half nuts engaged throughout the process.

## USING TAPS AND DIES

The alternative approach to screwcutting is to use taps (for internal threads) and dies (for external threads). But why cut threads by any other method than screwcutting? There are several reasons: it is inconvenient to cut metric threads on a machine with an imperial leadscrew (and vice versa) because, even if you have a translation gear, you can't use the thread dial indicator. Some special threads are even more difficult to cut on a lathe. Aside from 0BA (with a pitch of 1mm), the BA series has non-standard pitches in either system, which are difficult to achieve accurately without special changewheels. All small threads are difficult to cut on anything other than watchmakers or instrument lathes.

The alternative, using taps and dies, is often more practical. Plus, if you have a matching set of taps and dies, you can be sure threads cut with one will mate with the other. Unfortunately, when building a collection of tools, one of the significant areas of expenditure can be building a comprehensive set of taps and dies. A well-equipped model engineering workshop might have BA and metric sets, as well as *Model Engineer* ME taps in 40 and 32tpi, various Whitworth threads and perhaps several other types. With a full set of HSS BA taps and dies needing a significant investment, you could spend as much on taps as the cost of a mini-lathe. Many people find the most cost-effective route, or if not the least painful, is to acquire taps and dies as and when they are needed.

Those making larger models, workshop tooling or other bigger items are probably best starting with a good metric set. Beware economy carbon steel metric sets – these often are very poorly made, only have one or two taps per thread size and die nuts, which are often hexagonal. The latter are really only any good for restoring damaged threads and my experience of the taps is that they work but aren't very good. You can recognize them by their dull grey surface finish.

It is relatively easy to find 2mm to 12mm taps and dies in HSS (which will be a bright silvery colour) for very reasonable prices – so reasonable you may wonder if they are worth getting. The truth is that industry gets through these metric taps and dies by the container load, and quantity equals economy so we benefit from the savings. Although the dies are not split, you can expect them to produce good quality threads that will be a good fit in commercial nuts.

A metric set such as this will cover most of your day-to-day needs, allowing you to get on with the job in hand, and you can

fill in more esoteric sizes later. It's worth noting that, aside from the thread form (60 instead of 55 degrees), M6 is the same pitch and diameter as 0BA, M5 is a good substitute for 2BA and 3mm is close to 5BA. I don't mean you can use a 5BA nut on a 3BA screw but you can substitute the threads for each other in most applications. M2 lies between 8 and 9BA and may come in handy from time to time but is typically not included in these sets.

In the past, people often had 'half sets' of BA taps – sizes 0, 2, 4, 6, 8 and often 10. These six sizes will be enough for most small model making projects. If funds are tight, you could start with a decent carbon steel set and replace any breakages with HSS as you go along. If funds allow, a full set of eleven BA sizes is worth getting, particularly if most of your work is on small models. The alternative is a set in the smaller metric sizes.

Taps typically come in three types – taper, second and plug, also known as bottoming or, sometimes, finishing. Each tap has a progressively smaller taper on the end and they should be used in turn to create the thread.

Most of the new metric sets also have a significant difference in the outer diameter of the tap, so the second tap creates a 'tight' thread while the plug tap gives a looser fit (think how you can 'spin' a standard nut down a matching screw). Modern taps also often have grooves around the shank – one

for taper, two for second and none for the plug tap. This is a great help when trying to distinguish them in the smaller sizes.

Unlike taps, dies usually only come as one thread size but look at them carefully and you will see on one side there is a shorter 'lead' into the thread. Normally you cut threads with the side having the longest lead – usually, but not always, the side with writing on it. If you need to cut up to a shoulder, you can invert the die and this will allow you to squeeze in an extra turn or two of full thread.

Tapping holes in the lathe is straight-forward (Fig. 12.12). Simply hold the tap in the tailstock chuck, leave the tailstock 'loose' and take care not to overload the tap (push the tailstock along by hand and don't allow the tap to pull it along). It is often best to turn the spindle by hand, either with a mandrel handle or by just hauling the chuck around manually, but for coarser threads you can run the lathe very slowly and be ready to hit the e-stop. Start with the taper tap, anointing it with cutting fluid, and follow it with the second and plug taps to get an accurate thread.

All thread cutting can be improved by using a good lubricant. Good tapping oils and compounds (such as Trefolex and RTD) cope well under pressure and some are designed to cool the tool by evaporating as well as lubricating. Different people will swear by tallow, milk or even spit for

*Fig. 12.12 Threading a hole using a tap in the tailstock.*

different compounds. Others will argue for and against using a lubricant on cast iron. One thing most people agree on is that very light oils, even paraffin, are good for aluminium and that if using small taps in copper, use a proper tapping compound and great care!

Dies are more of a problem as they will not fit in the tailstock chuck and because they do not come in a series of three, progressively deeper, cuts they require more torque.

If you use a die 'freehand' with the work held in a vice it will often produce a thread that is rather wobbly. The ideal solution is a tailstock die holder (*see* Fig 12.14) but until you have one there is a satisfactory bodge. Take the tool-holder off the top slide to make some space and secure the tailstock so the spindle is a short way from the end of the work. Fit the die in an ordinary die holder and unplug the lathe. Now position the die ready to cut the thread and wind the tailstock spindle forward so it gently pushes on the die holder. Now use one hand to turn the chuck, while using the other to gently advance the tailstock spindle (Fig. 12.13). One arm of the die holder will rest on the top slide and you will start to cut a thread. The skill is to match the fairly hefty turning force needed on the chuck with light pressure from the tailstock. You may be surprised at how good the results are this way.

This does mean a certain amount of juggling and as mortals have, on average,

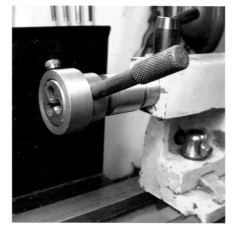

*Fig. 12.14 A simple tailstock die holder.*

two hands and none of us have three, sooner or later you will want to seek an easier solution.

The answer is a tailstock die holder. This is a cylindrical body with a recess for a different sized die at each end (Fig. 12.14). It is

*Fig. 12.15 Cutting a thread using the die holder.*

mounted on a tube or spigot attached to an arbor in the tailstock taper.

Make sure the item to be threaded is no more than, and ideally slightly less than, the top diameter of the thread to be cut. There is always some metal extrusion as well as cutting when making a thread and if the metal is dead on size (or over) the die will have to do a lot of unnecessary work. Chamfer the very end of the work a little to help start the die.

Unplug the lathe for die cutting. If you try to cut large threads under power the lathe will stall and blow a fuse. With small threads you might just mill the work down a few sizes instead. This is where a mandrel handle is useful, allowing you to turn the work slowly and under control but with good torque. Otherwise, just rotate the work by hand. Stop the die holder rotating by holding the tommy bar (Fig. 12.15). Use cutting fluid applied by brush and ideally take 'two steps forward, one step back' to keep the die clear. You might be able to just wind the die on to the work but your results may not be as good.

For the best results, you should start by sizing the die on a practice piece. Tighten the central screw so you start by cutting slightly oversize. Take a few trial cuts, gradually loosening the centre screw and tightening the outer screws, until an on-size nut is a suitable fit on the thread. You can now leave the die as it is and cut a series of perfect threads first time.

# 13 Milling in the Lathe

These days, it is not uncommon to find both a lathe and a milling machine in a typical hobby workshop but we all have to start somewhere and you are far more likely to purchase your mini-lathe as your first machine tool than to invest in a mill. This puts you in the same position as most hobbyists before the last decade or two of the twentieth century. They solved their milling problems using their lathes and a little ingenuity, and you can do the same.

In turning, the work revolves and the tool is held against it; in milling it is the cutter that rotates, hence the ability to carry out milling operations in the lathe doubles its applications. There are two approaches: the work can be held in the chuck and the tool mounted in a milling spindle (mounted on the toolpost) or the cutter can be mounted on the lathe mandrel and the work mounted on the cross slide. The crudest arrangement is to hold a cutter in a chuck and fix the work to the toolpost (Fig. 13.1) but there are more sophisticated approaches.

*Fig. 13.1 Even the simplest arrangement for milling in the lathe can tackle quite hefty jobs.*

A lathe offers similar levels of power to a mill but is arranged so the normal directions of traverse for the work are inappropriate. The answer to this conundrum is the 'vertical slide' (Fig. 13.2). This self-explanatory device adds a third dimension to the lathe. Combined with toolpost-mounted 'milling spindles' to effectively create a dual purpose machine, this was how almost all the model engineers of the past carried out their milling jobs.

There is a design of vertical slide produced for use with mini lathes (Fig. 13.3). This is unusual in having a built-in work clamp to which a separate milling table can be fixed. It is possible to use other designs of vertical slide, the small one produced for Taig/Peatol lathes, for example (Fig. 13.4). In order to get the most out of a small vertical slide on a mini-lathe you may need to use a raising block (Fig. 13.5) and you may also need to provide tapped fixing holes in the cross slide (Fig. 13.6). These should be positioned carefully to avoid interfering with the dovetails.

Lathes are designed, however, for cutting

*Fig. 13.2 Using a vertical slide adds the missing up and down movement.*

Fig. 13.3 A swivelling vertical slide made to suit mini-lathes.

Fig. 13.4 A smaller vertical slide often adapted for use with mini-lathes.

Fig. 13.5 A raising block can help get the most out of a small vertical slide.

forces in a single direction, so that the cross slide is pushed hard down on to the saddle and the saddle down on to the bed of the lathe. This gives rigidity even with enough play for the slides to move smoothly. In milling, the forces can be in any direction. They are also more likely to be interrupted as the teeth of the end mill bite into the work in turn. This means a greater chance of things slipping, more vibration and more risk of things going wrong.

There are two things we can do about this. The first is to make sure various slides are locked in place or at least tightened up

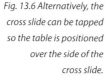

Fig. 13.6 Alternatively, the cross slide can be tapped so the table is positioned over the side of the cross slide.

more than usual. The second is to avoid climb milling. Climb milling is a technique where the work advances past the cutter in the direction where the cutter tries to pull the work under it (and so climb up over the work). It can work very well on rigid milling machines with little backlash but is a recipe for disaster on a relatively flexible lathe set-up. Always ensure you feed work against the direction of rotation of the cutter. This will give you a better finish and avoid any risk of the work being 'snatched' resulting in deep gouges or worse, such as a broken cutter.

## MILLING CUTTERS

In the past, plain cylindrical milling cutters were typically divided into two categories. End mills usually have four flutes and are used for cutting on their sides. Slot drills normally have two flutes and one of the end cutting edges is extended past the centre so it can be plunged into the work to create a hole. Slot drills also cut a slot to width more reliably.

Advances in grinding technology have seen the introduction of three- and four-flute cutters that can be plunged into the work, and the distinction between end mill and slot drill has been blurred. It remains the case that two- and three-flute cutters

*Fig. 13.7 The cutting edges of a pair of carbide end mills.*

*Fig. 13.8 A selection of FC3 'throwaway' mills.*

*Fig. 13.9 Plain and 'rippa' milling cutters.*

*Fig. 13.10 Home-made and bought T-slot and dovetail cutters.*

are more likely to cut a slot accurately to width but most modern cutters can happily be plunged into the work. If you are not sure, look closely at the end and see if one cutting edge is longer than the others (Fig. 13.7).

Just like lathe tools, both carbide and HSS milling cutters are available. Unlike with lathe tools, solid carbide milling cutters are generally very good but they are probably rather extravagant for lathe-based milling as they often give their best when removing red-hot chips! Sharpening milling cutters is more involved than sharpening lathe tools and could be the subject of an entire book.

A popular form of small cutter are the FC3 'throwaway' end mills, invariably in HSS (Fig. 13.8). These are designed for use by CNC machines, where they are used and then thrown away rather than resharpened. Always in small sizes, they either have a 6mm or ¼in shank, have either 'square' or round ends and are an inexpensive source of small cutters well suited to milling in the lathe. They are always ground to allow plunge cutting. The very smallest sizes are so small it is difficult to imagine how they are made and they need to be treated very gently. They can be resharpened with care (and a suitable tool grinder). In Fig. 13.8, you may see one small cutter has been broken

and resharpened as a single point cutter. This is probably the only way to restore the smallest cutters.

A mini-lathe has sufficient power to use larger end mills, easily up to 12mm (½in) diameter, although it is difficult to use such cutters at the sort of rates one might use in a proper milling machine (Fig. 13.9). Some milling cutters have 'notches' in their cutting edges. These 'rippa' type cutters produce

shorter chips and can remove material at a faster rate. This is unlikely to be a big issue for anyone milling in a lathe as the relative lack of rigidity of the set-up doesn't lend itself to heavy cuts.

As well as plain end mills, many other shapes are available. Two of the most common you may encounter or need are T-slot cutters and dovetail cutters (Fig. 13.10). Their uses should be obvious from their names. They are often rather large for use in a small lathe but can be used successfully if cuts are kept relatively modest and the feed rate is not excessive.

## FLY CUTTERS

A fly cutter is a single point tool, used usually for machining plane surfaces (Fig. 13.11).

The cutting point travels in a large circle and the work is traversed past it. In a lathe, this generally means holding the fly cutter in a chuck and mounting the work so it can be traversed using the cross slide.

*Fig. 13.12 With some experimentation it is possible to undertake most milling operations on the lathe.*

*Fig. 13.11 A simple fly cutter using an HSS toolbit.*

If the toolbit is a good one, rigidly held, a fly cutter will produce smooth, flat surfaces with the most basic of set-ups. It is also possible to fly cut convex surfaces but the lack of fine adjustment of the typical fly cutter imposes limits on accuracy. The downside is that, as fly cutters have a single cutting edge, usually at a large radius, they are very slow to use.

To hold milling cutters in the lathe the best solution is to use some form of collet system. The ER collet systems described in the chapter on workholding are probably the ideal solution for most users, combining effectiveness with modest cost. An alternative is to buy or make a simple one-size holder as described in the 'projects' section. One of these to take 6mm or ¼in shank cutters will suffice for most light milling projects carried out in the lathe.

Milling in the lathe is a huge topic and the possibilities for different set-ups and approaches are endless (Fig. 13.12). Although the cost of small benchtop milling machines has now come within the reach of many hobbyists, you will be surprised just how much you can achieve with your mini-lathe and a little ingenuity.

# 14 Modifications and Accessories for your Mini-Lathe

One of the benefits of a mini-lathe is the potential for increasing its flexibility, capabilities or ease of use by modifying it. This chapter details a series of changes that, even individually, can make a real difference to your use of the lathe. Some of them are very simple, others are relatively major exercises. Many owners have made multiple modifications to their mini-lathes, effectively turning them into custom machines that suit their workshop activities and ways of working.

Off the shelf upgrades are generally, but not always, straightforward and reversible. These usually require various parts that can be obtained from the better stocked suppliers, although it is often possible to make your own upgrade parts.

There are also many custom upgrades, some of which are not reversible. Owners of some venerable types of lathe are loathe to make any non-standard modification to their machines for fear of destroying their originality. While anyone whose machine is still under warranty may be justifiably cautious about making non-reversible alterations, a quick search on the internet will soon reveal a whole host of enthusiastic owners are quite happy to make even major changes.

## GUARDS

As mentioned in the safety section at the beginning of this book, guards that interfere with the use of the lathe are unlikely to be used. However, simple guarding from moving parts and flying swarf are important ways to protect both operator and machine.

Fig. 14.1 A simple shield from clear polycarbonate is possibly both the simplest and most effective guard.

The most effective guard is a simple rectangle of clear polycarbonate (not a relatively fragile acrylic sheet) attached to a heavy metal or magnetic base by a metal arm (Fig. 14.1). To be effective the supporting arm needs to be relatively rigid, so 10mm (⅜in) bar is ideal and is compatible with most easily available and relatively inexpensive magnetic bases. An ideal size is about 150mm × 200mm (6 × 8in). The great advantage of a guard such as this is it can be adjusted to give the maximum protection from sprays of chips or coolant and moved easily aside and replaced when, for example, you need to measure the work or to swap a chuck.

## TOOLPOST GUARD

The toolpost guard is an angled plastic shield that fits to the operator side of the top slide and particularly helps to protect the opera-tor when turning brass or similar metals that produce a shower of chips upwards from the tool (Fig. 14.2). These guards are available as an aftermarket kit of parts (Fig. 14.3). To mount the guard, two M6 holes have to be drilled and tapped in the top slide but this permits an arrangement that allows the guard to be swung clear of the toolpost in moments without any tools being required.

## LEADSCREW SWAP

Aside from the Micro-Mark lathes mentioned below, the only difference between a metric mini-lathe and an imperial one is the pitch of the leadscrew. On metric lathes it is 1.5mm pitch and on imperial lathes it is 16tpi. The only material difference this makes to the lathe is the ease of cutting metric or imperial threads so why, if a 63-tooth change gear can be used as a converter, bother changing the leadscrew?

*Fig. 14.2 For lathes fitted with a satisfactory chuck guard, a swing clear toolpost guard is an alternative solution to screening flying chips.*

*Fig. 14.3 The kit of parts that make up the swing clear guard.*

four small knurled knobs about 12mm (½in) in diameter with M5 screw holes (Fig. 14.4). Using Loctite or a similar retainer, fit about 10mm (⅜in) of M5 studding (or just the sawn-off ends of M5 screws) in each knob. You'll find these little thumbscrews are easy to fit single-handedly, even though you can't see behind the swarf guard. Attachment will now take only seconds so there's no excuse for not refitting it.

## QUICK RELEASE GEAR COVER

The answer is that as well as the leadscrew and clasp nuts, you also change the thread indicator dial. This allows you to disengage the clasp nuts when cutting threads from the same 'family' as the leadscrew and pick up the thread reliably.

## THUMBSCREWS FOR SPLASHGUARD

The rear splashguard has to be removed if you want to use the full travel of the cross slide or to remove the slide itself for any reason. Obviously, the splashguard has a valuable function in preventing swarf or coolant from heading behind the machine or getting to the motor so, if you have to remove it, you should work with care and replace it as soon as possible. The problem is it is held in place by small M5 cap head screws, which makes it almost impossible

to replace them without turning the lathe around as they keep dropping off the Allen key. This is very difficult if you have fixed it to the bench. A simple answer is to make

*Fig. 14.4 A simple exercise in turning, knurling and threading a set of M5 thumbscrews make removal of the splash guard much easier.*

The gear cover is held in place by two bolts. Removing and replacing these continually is tedious, yet the temptation to operate the lathe with the cover removed should

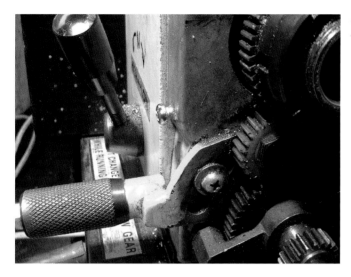

*Fig. 14.5 The rear gear cover fixing stud.*

be resisted for (hopefully) obvious reasons. Past solutions have involved replacing the M5 cap screws with an easier to release alternative, such as thumbscrews. However, this approach still means having to undo screws and there remains the risk of losing a fastener in the swarf or under the bench. As an alternative approach, it is a ten-minute job to perform an instant-release modification. However, it works only with those having the older-style gear cover, not the newer 'rectangular' C3 style.

Remove the guard retaining screws and identify and mark locations for two fixing lugs. These should be just above the bottom of the vertical sides of the reverse gear mounting plate. Drill the guard tapping size for M4 carefully. Replace the guard and, using a hand drill, spot through to the reversing gear mounting plate. Remove the gear plate, then drill and tap an M4 hole on each side of the plate at the spotted marks. Fit two round head screws (they do have a use!) in place, using retainer and leaving them 2mm from 'home' (Figs 14.5 and 14.6). Now open the holes in the cover up to 4mm and, with a razor saw or junior hacksaw, extend them into vertical slots (Fig. 14.7). The letters on the gear cover stand for forward, neutral and reverse.

It now takes only a moment to remove the cover with an up and out motion. Even

*Fig. 14.6 Both front and rear fixing studs are attached to the tumbler reverse mounting plate.*

*Fig. 14.7 Two vertical slots in the gear cover hook over the mounting studs. The letters F-N-R refer to the tumbler reverse.*

with the largest changewheels fitted, there is no interference and the guard is quite secure in normal use.

## METAL CHANGE GEARS

The change gears supplied with mini-lathes are made from nylon, aside from the two smallest 20-tooth gears. This allows a considerable saving over the cost of supplying metal change gears and, for most purposes, the nylon gears are perfectly adequate and are both accurate and quiet. Nonetheless, most lathes are supplied with metal change gears and it is possible to obtain full sets of either metric or imperial types to suit mini-lathes (Fig. 14.8).

*Fig. 14.8 Metal change gears are more robust than nylon ones and look good too.*

Metal gears are less tolerant of poor lubrication than nylon gears, so keep them lightly greased or oiled. They can also be noisier so, if noise is a problem, it is worth using a small piece of paper nipped between each pair of gears to set the clearance when setting up the train.

*Fig. 14.9 A thrust bearing under the toolpost clamp is a very simple way to reduce the force required for clamping.*

## TOOLPOST CLAMP BEARINGS

A very simple upgrade that can help reduce the force required to clamp the toolpost to the top slide securely is to fit a needle-roller thrust bearing under the clamp lever. The required size is a 10mm bore and these are available from some larger mini-lathe suppliers (Fig. 14.9). Be aware the bearings will probably mean the 'clamped' lever will point in a different direction. If this is an issue it is can be adjusted by taking a skim off the bottom of the lever's clamping surface.

## METAL KNOBS AND HANDWHEELS

I hesitate to classify this as an 'upgrade' as it is essentially a cosmetic exercise that won't make a significant difference to the performance of the lathe but it may well bolster your pride of ownership (Fig. 14.10). Sets are available with well-finished aluminium apron and tailstock handwheels with chrome handwheels and chromed ball-ended levers for the toolpost lock, tailstock barrel lock and the half nut engagement lever. Fitting time is quoted as about thirty minutes.

Many users think metal handwheels do improve the look and feel of the lathe, although some prefer the more contemporary look of the existing tapers levers to the ball-ended ones. This is, of course, entirely a matter of personal taste.

## ALTERNATIVE FEED SCREWS

The feed screws on most mini-lathes'top and cross slides have a pitch of exactly 1.00mm, not 25tpi, regardless of whether they are metric or imperial. An exception is the 7in × 14in mini-lathe available from Micro-Mark in the USA, which has trademarked True-Inch feed screws and dials. These have a pitch of 20tpi and fifty 0.001in divisions. An aftermarket conversion kit is available from the company that includes a new top slide.

## TWIN HALF NUTS AND THREAD INDICATOR DIAL

If you have a later mini-lathe with a single half nut and brace and do a lot of screwcutting, you may wish to benefit from the added convenience of a thread indicator dial and the added accuracy of a pair of half nuts. These are available from most stockists of mini-lathes but to fit them you will need to remove the leadscrew guard. It is, therefore, a good idea to fit an alternative guard as a replacement.

Fitting is easy enough and adjustment is simply as explained in the chapter on setting up the lathe. Be sure to order an indicator and half nuts to match your leadscrew – imperial or metric.

## DIGITAL FEED SCREWS

If you consider this change, it may be worth going the 'whole hog' and fitting the digital feed screw conversion kit that uses the same 20tpi feed screws but has digital readouts (Fig. 14.11, and fitted to the lathe in Fig. 14.10). Although the imperial feed screws are not available on their own in the UK, the digital ones are! Naturally, the advantage of digital feed screw readouts is they can read directly in metric and imperial with equal accuracy. Be aware they do not compensate for backlash, although this is rarely a problem on a lathe as one normally applies all cuts in the same direction.

*Fig. 14.10 A mini-lathe fully 'blinged up' with metal handwheels and levers and digital feed screw readouts.*

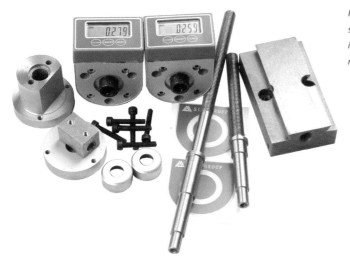

*Fig. 14.11 A digital feed screw conversion kit includes a new cross slide nut and top slide base.*

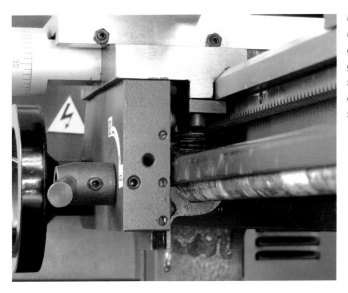

*Fig. 14.12 More recent mini-lathes are fitted with a full length leadscrew guard, and only have a single half-nut that closes against a leadscrew support bar.*

*Fig. 14.13 A simple plastic leadscrew guard made from plastic channel.*

## LEADSCREW SHIELD

Many recent mini-lathes are supplied with a full length 'shield' above the leadscrew, apparently due to requirements for leadscrews to be guarded (Fig. 14.12). This shield protects the leadscrew from swarf admirably but it means only a single half nut can be used to drive the saddle. If you have the earlier pattern with a two-part half nut, the advantages of finding a way to keep swarf off the leadscrew will be obvious. The worst area for swarf clogging the leadscrew is to the left, where it rains down from above during most machining operations.

A simple leadscrew guard can be made by cutting a piece of plastic electrical conduit or a similar channel-shaped material to fit over the leadscrew and hook loosely over the top clasp nut (Fig. 14.13). Although crude, this solution is surprisingly effective.

A more elegant solution is a proper metal shield. If you have attached an apron gear shield (*see below*), then the lower two screws holding the gear shield in place offer a way to fix a simple 1.5mm (¹⁄₁₆in or 16-gauge) aluminium shield over the leadscrew in this area (Fig. 14.14). The picture should be sufficient to guide anyone wishing to copy this simple device. None of the dimensions is critical, just ensure it does not interfere with the half nuts and it does not extend too far towards the headstock. The rim of the handwheel coming into contact with the control box cover is the limit on carriage movement, so by making the end of the shield level with it gives maximum protection with no lost movement. The shield may be extended temporarily with a second piece of aluminium with two 'ears' folded to grip the end of the fixed shield.

## APRON GEAR SHIELD

The carriage handwheel on the front of the apron is geared, via a pair of reduction gears, to a rack fitted to the front of the lathe bed. The overhang of the top of the lathe

*Fig. 14.14 A more sophisticated leadscrew guard folded up from aluminium sheet. The apron is inverted in this photograph.*

bed shields the rack from swarf. This does, however, quite easily find its way on to the gears, which are exposed at the back of the apron. They are difficult to clean because of their position and the swarf eventually finds its way on to the rack, causing distinct tight spots in its action.

The gears are set into the apron, so it is apparent immediately that covering the recess in which they lie can solve this problem. Unfortunately, the gears stand slightly proud of the recess is not sufficient, so a single flat plate is not sufficient. After removing the gears and handwheel, cut out two suitably shaped pieces of 2mm (³/₃₂in) acrylic sheet, using the apron as a template. Mark one piece so you can cut out a space to clear the gears – an easy task as the material

is transparent. Drill the other piece to clear the pinion that runs on the rack. After gluing the two pieces together, spot through them directly into the back of the apron for four holes. These can be tapped a suitable size such as M4 (Fig. 14.15).

Take the opportunity to anoint the gears with some grease and refit them. Finally, fix the shield in place with suitable screws. Ordinary cap head screws will do but slotted screws with broad, flat heads are ideal for holding a relatively fragile material such as acrylic. There is no reason why you can't use aluminium or any other sheet material that can be machined easily without splitting, it's just that a transparent material makes the job easier. Note that the larger gear protrudes from the top of the apron and shield into

a recess in the carriage but this is well out of the reach of swarf. One advantage of a transparent cover is you can easily see if any swarf has penetrated your defences!

## LONG BED

If you have a mini-lathe with one of the shorter bed lengths, you may find yourself wishing you had just that bit more space between centres. All is not lost, as you can buy a full length bed that gives 400mm (16in) between centres (if you are willing to let the tailstock overhang slightly). Changing the bed is not a particularly complex task as it is just a case of transferring each of the lathe's systems across. Aside from taking care to readjust everything properly in place on the new bed, the trickiest part is likely to be making sure you reattach the wiring harness correctly. As with any such process of disassembly and reassembly, it makes good sense to record your progress with digital photos.

## INCREASING CROSS SLIDE TRAVEL

Most lathe owners assume the cross-travel of their lathe's cross slide needs to be sufficient to face across the full diameter of the lathe's swing. In practice, this is rarely the case and, in all honesty, it is something we rarely need to do. There are exceptions, of course, such as truing up a faceplate but, more importantly, the more travel we have the greater flexibility we have in tool placement, making it easier to turn large diameters and bores or other awkward tasks.

For a mini-lathe, you might imagine the limiting factors on the cross slide travel of the machine are adequate engagement of the leadscrew in the feed nut and overlap of the dovetails. This is true when feeding the slide 'away from the operator' but, winding the saddle 'out', it will stop somewhat sooner than one might expect. It is, however, possible to increase the 'towards the operator' travel significantly. In fact, you

*Fig. 14.15 The apron gear shield is made from two layers of plastic sheet, the lower one cut out to clear the gears.*

*Fig. 14.16 A cross slide feed nut shaped to allow it to travel the full length of the slot in the saddle.*

*Fig. 14.17 A recess to clear the index dial allows maximum travel to be achieved.*

can increase the usable travel to more than 75mm (3in) with two minor modifications. The first step is to file the end of the feed nut to a radius of about 10mm (⅜in) so it can feed right up into the end of the slot in the saddle (Fig. 14.16). You will now find the slide butts up against the index, still limiting its travel. The next step is to mill or file a shallow recess in the saddle to clear the index (Fig. 14.17). Chamfering the bottom edge of the nut may be needed to ensure you get the last thou of full travel. Together this is quite a bonus as it gives about half an inch of extra travel and enables you to face work a full 6in diameter, as against about 5in as standard.

## BRASS GIB STRIPS

The slides on mini-lathes are made of cast iron that, unlike most metals, wears well in contact with other cast iron parts and is also a good bearing surface against steel. The gib strips fitted to a new mini-lathe

will be made of steel but one upgrade that is sometimes encountered is their replacement with hard brass gibs. These are claimed to offer 'smoother operating slides'. Having used a brass gib for a replacement T-slotted cross slide (Fig. 14.18), the author can testify to their good performance and this may well be a worthwhile investment for those seeking to achieve the very best performance from their machine.

*Fig. 14.18 A shop-made brass gib strip made for a T-slotted cross slide.*

## LEADSCREW GROMMET

At least one mini-lathe owner has 'lost' a controller board when a long snake of swarf found its way into the control box through the leadscrew hole and shorted out the board. Many modern mini-lathes now have a sealing grommet fitted around the leadscrew at this point and it is possible to obtain these as an aftermarket spare (Fig. 14.19). Alternatively, cut a suitable grommet

*Fig. 14.19 A simple sealing grommet can prevent swarf finding its way into the control box.*

from high density foam to fit around the leadscrew and glue it in place.

## FITTING A 100MM CHUCK

A small proportion of mini-lathes come ready fitted with a large flange for suitable 100mm (4in) chucks and it is possible to source replacement spindles with this larger flange. It may be worth considering this change at the same time as a bearing upgrade. The downside is that any chucks, faceplates or other accessories meant for the smaller flange can no longer be used. It is possible to fit such larger chucks to mini-lathes with a standard 80mm flange using a backplate. But first, what are the pros and cons of using larger chucks?

The obvious advantage is larger chucks can hold larger work; in particular the standard 80mm three-jaw chucks have quite limited capacity when using the inside jaws and a 100mm chuck is significantly bigger than you might assume (Fig. 14.20). A larger chuck allows you to hold many more workpieces with the inside jaws and the longer contact surface improves the hold general accuracy. However, all is not as simple as it seems, because when the jaws of a larger chuck are open fully there is a greater possibility of them fouling the slides when working near the chuck. This means a 100mm (4in) diameter chuck is probably the maximum practical size for a mini-lathe.

A second benefit is that a larger chuck has greater momentum. It weighs much more (a 100mm chuck and backplate weighs several times as much as an 80mm chuck) and the larger diameter also increases the 'flywheel effect'. This can mean that, especially on interrupted or difficult cuts, the lathe runs more smoothly and with less chatter when using a larger chuck.

The downsides are, of course, the extra weight hanging off the spindle and headstock and the greater bulk and overhang of the larger chuck. I understand SIEG does not specify the larger flange as standard because,

Fig. 14.20 A 25 per cent increase in diameter makes a 100mm chuck much larger than an 80mm chuck.

Fig. 14.22 The front of a pre-machined backplate, showing the register that fits the chuck.

Fig. 14.21 A 100mm chuck fitted to a mini-lathe.

although the generous bearings fitted to mini-lathes should be able to take the loads involved, concern has been expressed about the ability of the headstock casting to take the increased forces. The overhang issue is greatest for those with short-bed mini-lathes, particularly the smallest version with just 250mm (10in) between centres, which is distinctly cramped with a large chuck. On balance, however, there do not seem to be any negative reports from those who have fitted 100mm chucks to longer bed versions, including the author (Fig. 14.21).

To attach the larger chuck to the spindle, you need to fit a backplate. This is just a steel or cast iron disk that fits between the flange and the chuck with suitable registers front and back. Fully machined backplates are available for some chucks (Fig. 14.22) but for others you may have to buy a part-machined backplate. The part-machined type can be mounted on the flange and then a spigot turned on the front to match the recess on the chuck. You may need to fit three or four M6 studs (M6 cap screws with the heads cut off can be used) to the backplate if none is supplied with it. They should be kept in place in the backplate with a suitable thread-locking compound.

The chuck should be supplied with a recommended depth and diameter of spigot. Start by rough turning the spigot about 2mm (¹⁄₁₆in) oversize. Using a sharp HSS tool, turn the very end of the spigot until it just enters the back of the chuck with no shake. Once you have a good, snug fit, set the cross slide index to zero and turn down the rest of the spigot. If you remove too much off the diameter accidentally, face the spigot off and try again – there is usually plenty of spare metal (too much, some would say) in these backplates. To complete the task, you will need to drill three or four holes for the chuck mounting screws. These can be marked out, spot drilled and opened out in a drill press. The holes should be somewhat oversize so the chuck is located only by the spigot and not by the screws. An advantage of turning the backplate in place is the spigot is guaranteed to be concentric with the spindle, giving the chuck the best possible opportunity to show its quality.

It's worth remembering that, if you get the opportunity to pick up a good quality chuck, either new or in good second-hand condition, it is possible to mount most types on a suitable backplate.

## SPINDLE SPEED READOUTS

Only a relatively small proportion of brushed motor mini-lathes have a built-in speed readout. Some SIEG-manufactured

*Fig. 14.23 For lathes with a suitable senor and socket fitted, adding a tachometer is simply a case of plugging it in.*

mini-lathes with brushless DC motors do, however, have a socket on the control panel that allows a speed readout to be plugged in (Fig. 14.23). Connecting the readout is not difficult but placement of the unit, which is on a cable, needs a little care. The readout boxes have built-in magnets that can be used to mount them on the headstock but the cable can decide to take an awkward path in front of the control panel.

## FITTING A QUICK CHANGE TOOLPOST

A quick change toolpost (QCTP) is one of those accessories you never knew you

needed but once you have one you will not know how you managed without it (Fig. 14.24). Several of the photos in this book feature the author's shop-made QCTP. There are various styles available but they all work on the same basic principle. A solid body is fitted to the toolpost stud in the place of the usual four-way toolpost. The body will have some sort of dovetails or other guides to locate changed tool-holders easily and a means for locking them in place. The tool-holders have adjustable stops to ensure they are the right height for each tool – no more shims! When choosing a toolpost, make sure when it is fitted it will

be possible to set tools low enough so they will be at centre height. This usually means the holders must overhang the toolpost mounting block.

Imagine a repeat job that requires several tool changes, more than can be conveniently fitted to the four-way toolpost. This means fiddling with shims, adjusting the height of tools and having to allow for changes in the amount by which they protrude from the holder. In contrast, with a QCTP you just loosen off the clamp, lift off one tool in its holder, drop in another and lock the clamp again.

It is possible to obtain several types of tool-holder. There are simple ones that just clamp square tool steel or the shanks of tipped tools, parting tool-holders or ones with circular sockets for round tools. More complex ones include knurling tools, holders for measuring equipment and Morse taper sockets. When choosing a QCTP, it is worth making sure a good range of tool-holders are available and also that they are reasonably priced.

Fitting a QCTP to a mini-lathe is usually quite simple if you obtain a lathe-specific toolpost you simply remove the old toolpost and clamp the new one in place. It is quite practical to fit other types of QCTP to mini-lathes, just make sure the tool-holders do not overlap the top slide and they can be lowered sufficiently to place tools at centre height. If you obtain a non-standard QCTP, you may find its central bore is a poor fit on the toolpost stud. On rare occasions the bore may be less than the required 10mm diameter, in which case check it is possible to drill or bore it out to 10mm without damaging the mechanism. It is rather simpler to deal with an oversized central hole. All that is required is a tubular spacer that can be either left loose or kept in place with a retainer. Its length ought to be slightly less than the height of the holder body.

It is quite practical to make your own quick change toolpost, with the advantage that you can also make your own tool-

*Fig. 14.24 A quick change toolpost market for mini-lathes with three tool-holders.*

*Fig. 14.25 A shop-made QCTP in use on the author's mini-lathe.*

holders in whatever quantity and styles you wish (Fig. 14.25).

## FITTING IMPROVED BEARINGS

Fitting higher specification bearings is probably the most involved of all the 'off-the-shelf' modifications. Many users who make this upgrade report a dramatic improvement in parting off, particularly from the point of view of being able to speed up and increase the depth of cut. You may also find the lathe will run more smoothly at low speed and notice a welcome change in the quality of surface finish on tougher materials. For a day's effort and at modest cost, the results can be really surprising. Even with a lathe that appears to be performing well with the standard ball bearings, you might consider changing to angular contact or roller bearings and taking full advantage of the basic precision and rigidity of the mini-lathe design.

### Angular Contact or Taper Roller?

In principle, good quality taper roller bearings offer the most accurate solution for a lathe mandrel and are used on most high quality precision lathes. They are slightly bulkier than angular contact bearings and this makes fitting them more involved.

Angular contact bearings are still greatly superior to deep groove bearings as they resist longitudinal loads better and can be adjusted to give very accurate running.

On the face of it, replacing the existing ball bearings is straightforward – strip down the mandrel, remove the old bearings, lubricate and fit the new ones and re-assemble. In practice, there are a few complications; in particular the bearings are a press fit in their housings and therefore a number of special tools are needed or will have to be improvised (Figs 14.26 and 14.27). Fitting taper roller bearings is the most involved procedure and fitting angular contact bearings is an

*Fig. 14.26 An improvised puller extracting the spindle of a mini-lathe.*

identical process, except it is not necessary to modify any spacers or shields as they have the same external dimensions as the standard bearings. Unlike the standard ball bearings, which are shielded units, roller bearings are open and in two parts – an outer race and the inner race with caged rollers attached. Overcome the temptation of taking the bearings out of their packaging before fitting them. If you can't, keep them clean and do not run them 'dry'.

Full details of how to make an angular contact bearing change can be found online at www.arceurotrade.co.uk/machineguides/Mini-Lathe-Angular-Contact-Bearing-Change-Guide.pdf.

### Fitting a Large Flange Spindle

The procedure for fitting a large flange spindle suitable for 100mm (4in) chucks is essentially the same as a bearing change. For the modest additional expense it is almost certainly worth upgrading the bearings at the same time, especially as they will be better able to handle the higher loads associated with larger chucks. Do be aware the larger flange will render the lathe unsuitable for use with many standard accessories – you may be better off using a larger chuck with a backplate.

*Fig. 14.27 A bearing removed using a slide hammer.*

## FITTING METAL OR REPLACEMENT NYLON HEADSTOCK GEARS

If you have a sudden jam-up of a brushed motor mini-lathe, it is quite possible one or more of the gears in the headstock will strip. It is also possible to obtain replacement gears fairly cheaply or to 'upgrade' the gears to metal ones (Figs 14.28 and 14.29). Be aware that metal gears may be somewhat noisier than nylon ones. Also, in the event of another 'crash', something other than the gears may give way.

## Replacement

The procedure for changing the gear pair on the spindle is effectively the same as for changing the bearings, although you don't have to remove the bearing or shield from the front of the spindle. There is also another gear pair on a layshaft supported in ball bearings beneath the spindle. This is easier to remove but requires the headstock to be removed and a C-clip on one end of the shaft to be released. The layshaft can then be pressed out gently and the gear pair will slip off. This gear pair is the one moved by the high/low gear lever so ensure the fork on the lever is engaged properly between the gears on reassembly and is well lubricated. Although this second gear pair slides on its layshaft, it is keyed to it so the shaft rotates in the bearings. Take care not to lose the key. Some mini-lathes have an encoder disc for a tachometer on the spindle so take care not to damage it.

## Running In

After fitting metal gears, ensure they are lubricated with a suitable grease. It is particularly important to ensure metal gears are 'run in'. Put the machine in low gear and allow the lathe to run at a modest speed for several minutes without any load, then gradually spin it up to top speed over ten or fifteen minutes. Stop the machine and change to high gear and repeat the process. You may wish to check the gears are still well lubricated afterwards, even though this means removing the headstock again.

*Fig. 14.28 A view inside the headstock of a brushed motor mini-lathe showing the nylon gears.*

*Fig. 14.29 A metal replacement for a nylon headstock gear.*

# 15 Projects

This chapter covers a number of practical projects that can give you some practice in using the lathe.

## PROJECT: ENDMILL HOLDER

A basic endmill holder makes a simple project that is an excellent introduction to thread cutting and simple turning and also extends the versatility of the lathe (Figs 15.1 and 15.2). While it is possible to hold milling cutters in the chuck, a proper cutter holder gives much better results. Many cutters have a threaded shank to fit special collets but the smaller sizes are available with plain shanks. These are usually 6mm for metric sizes and ¼in for imperial sizes. These are precision tools and should be held in a holder that matches their accuracy. It is not difficult to make one of these from a suitable 'blank arbor' – MT3 arbors to fit the lathe mandrel taper, with easily machined 25mm (1in) diameter sections on the end are available readily.

With a little care, it is possible to achieve an accurately centred hole that is a close

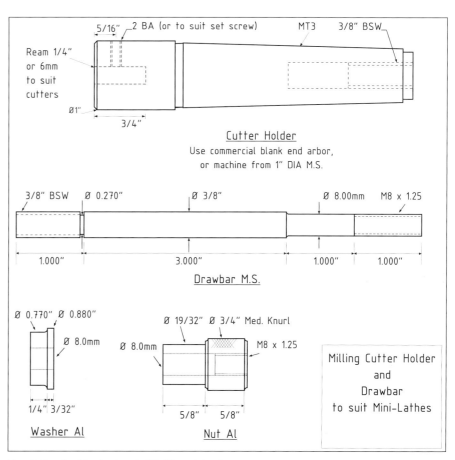

Fig. 15.2 Details of the simple endmill holder and drawbar.

Fig. 15.1 The simple endmill holder in action.

sliding fit for the cutters. Check the lathe is switched off. Remove the chuck from the lathe by unscrewing the three nuts and clean out the taper in the end of the mandrel with a tapered piece of wood, *not* a finger. The MT3 arbor should slip in securely, with a gentle twist to lock it in place. Use the tailstock drill chuck to make an accurate hole in the end of the arbor to suit your mills.

Start with a well-lubricated centre drill followed by an intermediate drill to full depth. Minimizing the extension of the tailstock barrel and 'almost locking' its movement both help to achieve a good result. Then drill several thou undersize, before reaming to the exact size. If you prefer to use metric cutters you will need to aim for a final size of 6mm, so start by drilling out to, ideally, 5.8mm. For ¼in, a letter C drill is ideal, or

¹⁵⁄₆₄in at a push. Finish by reaming to size with a machine reamer. Look for good tailstock alignment, the right amount of material to remove, keep the speed rather slower than for drilling and use some cutting fluid. Apply the latter with a brush or oilcan, you don't need a continuous flow. Make the cut with steady pressure.

If you haven't got a suitable reamer, you can make a D-bit from a piece of 6mm or ¼in silver steel that is ground, then hardened and tempered, and the tip lightly reground (Fig. 15.3). In use, a D-bit works like a slow drill. Keep it well lubricated, feed it in slowly and it will produce a remarkably accurate hole.

To lock the cutters in place, a radial hole for a set screw is needed. Either M5 or 2BA will suit. Drill the hole on the drill press with the arbor held in a vice, then tap it as squarely as you can. A centre pop will help ensure the drill does not 'skid' on the surface. This screw engages with a flat on the shank of the mill.

*Fig. 15.3 A selection of D-bits.*

Milling cutters tend to vibrate and also 'grab' more readily than drills. This could pull the taper from its socket with disastrous results for the work and the cutter. The solution is a drawbar, a rod screwed into the end of the holder and tightened against a stop at the far end of the mandrel. You can improvise a drawbar from M10 or ⅜in BSW studding (to suit the thread on your arbor) with a

suitable nut and washer. However, making a 'proper' drawbar is a good practice job.

## Drawbar

Start with a suitable length of 10mm (or ⅜in) steel bar. Put about 25mm (1in) of the appropriate thread to suit the arbor on the end (Fig. 15.4), following the directions in Chapter 12 on screwcutting. Now turn the drawbar end for end and turn down the last two inches to just under 8mm diameter. The next job is to cut a thread on this reduced section. Use an M8 die and cut about 25mm (1in) of thread.

The next item is a simple plug to fit the

*Fig. 15.4 Testing the drawbar thread in the arbor.*

*Fig. 15.5 The components of the finished holder and its drawbar.*

end of the mandrel, although the diameters are fairly critical. The plug must be an easy fit in the mandrel, with a larger shoulder that just fits through the hole in the lathe's gear cover. The rounded tool is useful as the end of the mandrel has a slight internal chamfer and the curved shoulder fits this nicely.

The nut completes the components of the drawbar and holder (Fig. 15.5). Start with a slightly over-length piece of ¾in round stock. Aluminium alloy is adequate for this job, although brass or mild steel could be better. Face the end and turn down the shank of the nut. Start a hole with a centre drill and drill right through at tapping size for an 8mm thread, 7.0mm is close enough, letter K or ⁹⁄₃₂in. Now open out the bore to 8mm for roughly half its depth (use insulation tape around the drill bit as a depth gauge) and lightly chamfer the sharp edges.

Turn the nut end for end in the chuck and face it smooth. Once again, turn off the lathe. Turning the chuck by hand, tap the nut 8mm with a tap in the tailstock chuck. Now assemble the plug and nut on to the drawbar and hold the drawbar in the chuck to allow you to knurl the nut. If you don't have a knurling tool, the hole for a tommy bar alone will be fine.

Finally, use the rounded tool again to trim off the first sixteenth or so of pattern from each end of the knurl and get a truly professional result.

You are now ready to set up a milling cutter. Fit one into the holder and secure it with the grub screw. Remove the chuck and check the taper socket is clean with a piece of wood. Push the taper into the socket with a gentle twisting motion – aim for a secure fit that won't pull out with a gentle tug but don't force it in or use anything other than finger pressure. Thread the drawbar in through the end of the mandrel and screw it into the end of the holder. Assemble the plug and nut on to the drawbar, doing them up securely enough to stop the taper slipping under vibration or if the cutter 'grabs' the work.

## PROJECT: A FLY CUTTER

There are various ways of making a fly cutter. The basic requirement is simply a toolbit holder that is easy to attach to a rotary machine such as a lathe or a mill and presents a cutting edge that travels in a circle around the axis of the lathe. This straightforward but useful design is similar to many commercial items and uses a square section HSS tool (Fig. 15.6). Another useful style is in the form of a tool-holder that bolts directly to the faceplate.

The body of the cutter is just a piece of

*Fig. 15.6 A simple flycutter to take ¼in HSS toolbits.*

25mm (1in) mild steel bar, turned down to 12mm (½in) to make the shank. This means when the cutter is held in a chuck, the body can be held flush against the jaws, preventing any rearward movement. The thick end of the bar can be sawn and then filed (or milled) to a 10 degree angle. The tool slot follows this angle to give the toolbit relief.

For use with 6mm (¼in) HSS tool steel, a slot offset so one side runs along the centre line of the body is needed. On a mini-lathe,

you can cut this slot by holding the shank in the lathe's tool-holder, turned through 10 degrees. Cut the slot with a suitable slot drill – an FC3 mini-mill of the same size as the tool steel will give a slot that is good fit. By 'plunging' the cutter into the thick side of the body, two recesses for tapped holes for the securing screws are made easily. M4 (or 4BA) screws are suitable for a small holder such as this.

The critical exercise is making a good toolbit. Start with a roughly 50mm (2in) long piece of square HSS. If you need to shorten a longer piece, grind a shallow groove all round using a mini-drill and carborundum wheel or similar. Hold the bar in a vice covered with a cloth, then tap the end sharply with a hammer.

To visualize the shape of the tool, think how it will contact the work as it rotates. With the bit in the holder, identify the corner that will do the cutting. The shape is identical to a right-handed knife tool. The angle of the holder helps provide one clearance angle but you need to grind further clearance on the end, 'front' and 'top' of the bar. Aim for 5-10 degrees of relief front and top and about 15 degrees on the end of the bar.

In use, the cutter should be held firmly in a chuck (Fig. 15.7). Fly cutters need to

*Fig. 15.7 Using the fly cutter on an aluminium plate.*

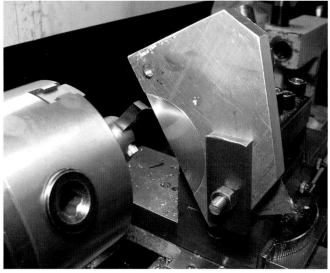

be run slowly; this one has a maximum of a 75mm (3in) cut and you should run it no faster than you would turn a bar of this size, perhaps about 100rpm when cutting mild steel. The work should be moved past the cutter. On mini-lathes, it can be a challenge to achieve a set-up where the whole area to be worked passes the cutter unless you have a vertical slide. The depth of cut and feed rate should be less than you would use for turning because of the significant leverage between the end of the cutter and the shank. However, if you are patient and keep your cutters sharp you will get excellent results.

## PROJECT: A SADDLE STOP

The principle of a saddle stop is simple but it offers a powerful aid to anyone wishing to make several parts of the same size and also has a few other uses. Basically, the stop is a moveable clamp that fits to the lathe bed, with a screwed bar for fine adjustment, that provides a fixed and repeatable location to which the lathe saddle can be advanced. If the top slide is used in conjunction with the stop this sets a datum point that can be used for multiple cuts at repeatable locations. Ready-made saddle stops are available for mini-lathes (Fig. 15.8) but making your own is a simple and satisfying project (Fig. 15.9).

Fig. 15.8 A commercially available saddle stop.

Fig. 15.9 A shop-made saddle stop.

## Stop Body

The challenge with making a reliable stop is to ensure a good fit to the lathe bed so it does not slip, yet does not need to be clamped with too much force. Mini-lathes have an 'inverted V' at the front of the bed that aligns the headstock, saddle and the tailstock. This provides an obvious location for the body of the stop and the body is just

a short length of steel bar with a cutout to fit over the V (Fig. 15.10).

The sides of the V are at 90 degrees to each other and at 45 degrees to the lathe bed (Fig. 15.11). The easiest way to machine the stop to fit them is to mount the steel blank for the body at 45 degrees and mill the cut-out using an end mill or slot drill. As the top of the V has a flat on it, it isn't essential to take the slot out of the middle of the cut-out so I haven't shown this on the drawing. If you lack milling facilities, you can clamp an over-size blank to the side of the toolpost and mill the V in the lathe. If you'd rather not do this, there is no reason why you can't saw and file the cut-out. The various other surfaces can be finished in any way you choose, including holding the body in a four-jaw chuck and facing them flat. Whichever way you choose to make this part, take care to get a good fit and finish on the V so the clamp does not damage the lathe bed.

The two holes in the body are straightforward. The one for the stop bar is threaded M6, and the other is M5 clearance, counterbored

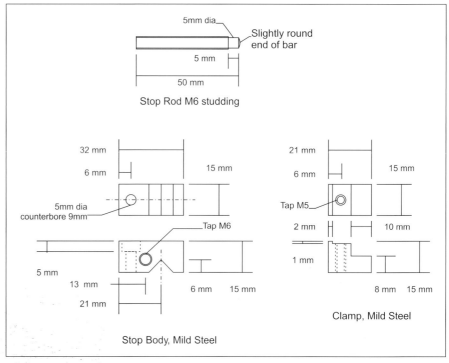

Fig. 15.10 Details of the saddle stop.

Fig. 15.11 The 'V' that locates on the lathe bed.

for the head of an Allen screw. The drawings show plenty of clearance between the two holes for simplicity.

### Clamp

The clamp piece fits below the body and presses against the lower surface of the bed where the saddle gib bears. The top of the clamp needs a raised section along its outer edge, as shown in the drawing. This provides a pivot that generates a positive clamping action. The dimensions given should work well but if you do not get adequate clamping with fairly gently tightening of the M5 screw, reduce the height of the clamp slightly.

### Stop Bar

The stop bar itself is simply a piece of threaded studding with the 'business end' neatly finished and a locking nut fitted. Try to dome the end of the bar slightly. With the dimensions given it will bear against a flat, machined area on the saddle. Keep it to the specified length and you will not have to remove the stop fully when it is not in use as you can loosen it off and slide it to the extreme left of the bed.

### In Use

To use the stop, advance the saddle to an appropriate point and fix the stop with the end of the bar hard against it (Fig. 15.12). You can adjust the rod for different locations or simply loosen off the clamp and move the whole stop according to your preferences. Make sure the locking nut is done up against the body as this ensures the rigidity essential for repeatability. With the saddle in approximate position, you can use the top slide to set the tool in an exact position and zero the index in case you need to make any other cuts relative to this starting datum. A stop like this can be easily repeatedly accurate to within a thousandth of an inch.

Fig. 15.12 The saddle stop in use.

Another use is ensuring the tool is always advanced to exactly the same point when boring a blind hole or a flange. Instead of listening for chatter as the tool approaches the bottom of the hole, you can just gently wind it in up to the stop and be confident of getting a reasonably flat-bottomed hole. With many designs of boring tool, once you have the hole to size, winding the boring tool into the centre while still at the stop will give a good finish to the bottom of the hole.

Don't rely on the stop as a safety feature. It may help stop you running the saddle into the chuck but this only works under manual feed – you should not expect it to stop the saddle if it is under power feed.

### PROJECT: MANDREL HANDLE

Despite the versatility afforded by electronic speed control, there are many jobs that benefit from the ability to turn the work by hand. These include cutting threads that are very short or run up to a shoulder and using taps and dies. For some jobs, such as tapping a hole, it is possible to turn the chuck or faceplate by hand. The construction of mini-lathes does not give the time-honoured option of pulling a drive belt, at least not in any practical fashion. In any case, more force or control is often required, for example when threading up to a shoulder. The classic solution to this problem is a handle that fits in the end of the headstock mandrel, an excellent accessory for any small lathe and yet one that is almost never offered as a commercial item (Fig. 15.13).

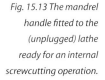

Fig. 15.13 The mandrel handle fitted to the (unplugged) lathe ready for an internal screwcutting operation.

To ensure the handle does not slip, it is usual to use some form of expanding collet. Usually this relies on the flexing of a narrow neck to allow the collet segments to expand. This has two disadvantages. Firstly, unless the neck is quite long, the collet does not grip along its length, increasing the clamping force required. Secondly, this usually means quite a long collet, typically three or four inches. This is a disadvantage when the workpiece itself extends into the mandrel bore or if you wish to mount a taper in the mandrel. This design uses a shorter 'floating collet' in order to achieve parallel expansion, giving excellent grip with a relatively short extension into the bore (Fig. 15.14). The handle can be attached and removed in a few seconds, with or without the gear cover in place.

**The Floating Collet**

The basic function of the handle relies on a two-piece collet that expands as a matching taper is drawn into it. To get the 'floating' action, the 'small' ends of the collet jaws locate in a ring (which itself locates in the end of the mandrel) and a circular spring holds the two jaws gently in place.

Turn the collet and its locating ring from a 2in offcut of a 25mm (1in) mild steel bar, starting by reducing a 35mm (1⅜in) length to 20mm (0.790in) diameter, which is sufficient to make the collet and the inner lip of the locating ring. This is one of the few critical dimensions and should be a 'running fit' in the mandrel – too tight and it will be difficult to assemble on to the lathe and remove again, too loose and the contact area of the collet will be insufficient to grip well. Using a parting tool, cut a groove to a depth of 0.90mm (0.035in) 25mm (1in) from the end and at least 3.2mm (⅛in) wide. This will be the end of the collet that locates in the cup.

The next task is to centre, drill and ream 8mm (⁵⁄₁₆in) for the spindle. Take care to ensure concentricity, once again aiming for a close fit. Using a square ended parting

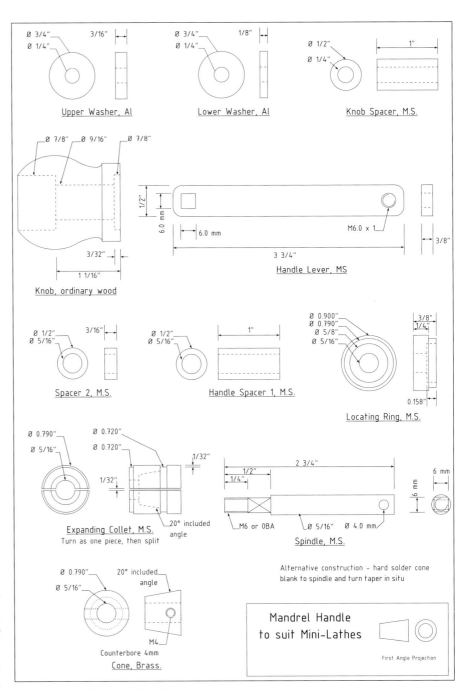

Fig. 15.14 Details of the mandrel handle.

tool, cut a groove to suit your circular spring. A search through various bunches of keys should produce several potential candidates. Choose one that is relatively light and quite round. The groove needs to be deep enough for the spring not to protrude at all.

You now need a small boring tool that will enter the 8mm (⁵⁄₁₆in) hole. There are few commercial bars this small but one ground like a D-bit from 6mm (¼in) HSS will do the job. See Chapter 8 on tooling for details.

Set the tool at centre height and angle the top slide at 10 degrees. This is done

*Fig. 15.15 Hollowing out the taper collet.*

*Fig. 15.16 Turning the cone to a fine finish.*

by winding the slide all the way back to access its two fixing screws. No great accuracy is needed, as long as you don't alter the setting between turning the collet and cone. Remember the angle dial on the slide is only approximate – always use an angle gauge or a try square if you need to set the slide more accurately. Use the top slide to work the tool in and out of the hole, advancing the cut by winding out the cross slide (Fig. 15.15). If you made the blank to the given dimensions, then reduce the thickness of the rim of the hole to a little less than 1mm (about ⅟₃₂in). To get the depth accurate, adjust the saddle so the tool is at the correct depth when the ends of the top

slide are aligned and set the index to zero. As you cut the taper, watch the end of the slide and, as the ends near alignment, take the index wheel round to zero at the end of each cut.

Now remove the work from the chuck and put a short piece of 20mm (¾in) diameter brass or mild steel in its place. Drill and ream to 8mm (⁵⁄₁₆in) and then, using an ordinary knife tool, form the taper at the same setting of the top slide as before (Fig. 15.16). It may take a little fiddling but if the tip angle of the tool is acute enough you should be able to set it so it can cut the taper without needing a run out groove cut in the bar. Try to get a nice smooth finish on the cone. A small flat

on the tool tip will help with this. Now test the collet and cone on an 8mm (⁵⁄₁₆in) rod. They should fit one another perfectly but the cone must not fully enter the collet. If it does bottom out, face a little off the end of the cone. Part off the cone.

Replace the collet piece in the chuck and, using an engineer's square, re-align the top slide. Now part off the collet, leaving a short shoulder at the end. Face the end of the remaining stub so a 3mm (⅛in) length of the shoulder remains. Using the boring bar, cut a recess just over 3mm (⅛in) deep and an easy fit for the small end of the collet. Part off the completed locating ring. Finish the collet by carefully hacksawing it in two. To mark this out accurately, clamp the collet to a flat surface and scribe a line around it using a surface gauge set to half its diameter. If you haven't got a surface gauge, use a suitable depth of packing as a guide for a scriber.

## Spindle

The spindle is simply a length of 8mm (⁵⁄₁₆in) rod, turned down to 6mm for 10mm (⅜in). Thread this final portion M6 (using a die is fine), then mark off a further 10mm (⅜in). Hold the rod in a bench vice to file this section square. This can be done surprisingly accurately by eye. Start each section by filing at the 'thick' end, then gradually widen it out, aiming to make the two edges of the surface parallel. Once the flat surface is about 6mm (nearly ¼in) wide, file the opposite side, then the last two sides, aiming to leave a small 'land' of the original surface of the rod between each face of the square.

The cone can now be fixed to the end of the spindle with a high strength retainer. This will be plenty strong enough as long as the spindle is a close fit in its hole. Alternatively, the cone can be fixed by pinning through a cross-hole, as shown on the drawings, or silver soldered in place.

Make the handle lever from a 90mm

(3¾in) length of 12mm × 5mm (½in × ³⁄₁₆in) steel bar. One end needs to be tapped M6. At the other end, drill a 6mm hole, then open this out to a square to fit the square section on the spindle. You will find it is easier to use a triangular section file than a square one for this job. You can fit a wooden knob to the end of the handle or alternatively make a smaller knob from brass bar. The washers and spacer are straightforward enough. You have now made all the components of the handle (Fig. 15.17).

Figure 15.18 shows how the parts fit together. With the collet slack and the lathe unplugged, push the collet into the end of the mandrel and tighten the spindle nut. You should need little force to get a very firm grip. With the dimensions given, the handle should comfortably clear the changewheel gear cover. Removal of the handle is simple – loosen the nut to the end of the thread and tap it lightly to loosen the collet.

A further improvement that can be made to this design is to fit the nut with a handle (Fig. 15.19) or make a short handle, say 35mm (1½in) long, with an M6 tapped hole in it. This will make tightening and loosening the handle very easy and not require the use of a separate spanner.

**Safety Note**

Please remember this handle is solely for use with the lathe isolated from its supply. Even running slowly, the handle will unbalance the lathe and, worse still, present a major threat to fingers and other extremities as it whirls around. Get in the habit of disconnecting the lathe by pulling the plug before fitting the handle and removing the handle before powering on again.

Fig. 15.17 The component parts of the finished handle.

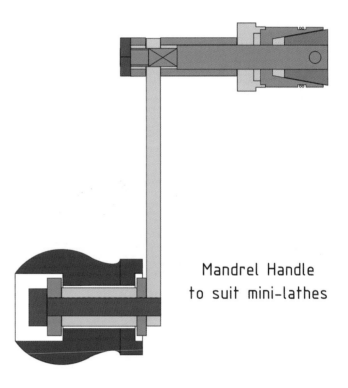

Fig. 15.18 An assembly diagram for the handle.

Mandrel Handle to suit mini-lathes

Fig. 15.19 The finished handle with modified lever nut.

# 16    Where Next?

If you have got this far, it is likely you have decided to get a mini-lathe. Hopefully you will find it a reliable and flexible tool that will get you off to a good start in model or hobby engineering. You may now be thinking 'what next?' There are perhaps three main paths that people with an interest in engineering as a hobby follow:

## MODEL ENGINEERING

Model engineering covers a huge field. Many people will associate it with live steam, especially model locomotives, but all manner of steam engines – stationary (Fig. 16.1), traction engines and marine engines – and internal (and external!) combustion engines make great subjects for modelling, as do electrical locos (Fig. 16.2), cars and all manner of other subjects (Fig. 16.3). Traditionally, model engineering also encompasses clock making and instrument making, such as microscopes and orreries, although these are, of course, 'full size'.

If this sort of challenge is your interest, I suggest you attend a model engineering show or an open day at a local model engineering club. It is the best way to get a feel for the sorts of project you might take on and also provides a chance to talk to people and find out what is involved. Joining a local club is also a great way to get practical advice when you are starting out. Another source of inspiration is *Model Engineer* magazine, which has been supporting the hobby since 1898!

Fig. 16.1 A model of a Victorian stationary steam engine.

Fig. 16.2 A 3½in gauge diesel outline loco.

Fig. 16.3 A model grass roller.

Fig. 16.4 A shop-made boring head.

*Model Engineers' Workshop.*
Naturally, this is a crude classification and many other lathe owners may use their machine to support hobbies as varied as boat-making, aero modelling, archery, gun-making or fishing.

Whatever you choose to do, like the author, you may find your mini-lathe remains your companion for many years and continue to modify and tweak it to suit your interests and needs (Fig. 16.6). Alternatively, you may find your horizons are different and that you end up changing it for a different machine, perhaps much larger. If you do, you will find the basic skills you acquired on your mini-lathe will stay with you and can be carried across, even to much bigger machines. Whatever path your hobby takes you on, I hope the time you spend at your mini-lathe is as fruitful and rewarding as mine has been. Work safely but, above all, enjoy your hobby!

## VEHICLE RESTORATION AND CUSTOMIZATION

A surprisingly large proportion of hobby engineers put their energy into restoring cars and, particularly, motorcycles. This includes making kit cars and even building entire vehicles from the tyres up! If this is your choice, you are likely to need a larger lathe at some point but even a mini-lathe can be useful for making specialist components.

## WORKSHOP PROJECTS

Some hobbyists end up spending most of their spare time making tools to make tools! Their reward is in meeting the challenges of making practical hard-working tools (Fig. 16.4). You may want to make further improvements to your mini-lathe (Fig. 16.5) and, again, a visit to a club or model engineering show can provide inspiration. However, sadly less home-made workshop equipment has been exhibited in recent years, despite this aspect of the hobby being very popular. The magazine for those most interested in tools and techniques is

Fig. 16.5 A T-slotted cross slide for the mini-lathe.

Fig. 16.6 The author's mini-lathe as it is today, much modified including a conversion to three-phase variable frequency drive.

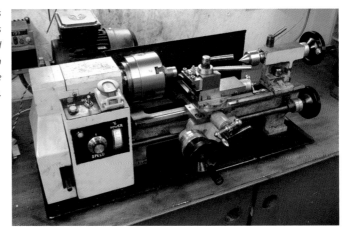

# *Further Information*

## Books

Relatively few books have been written about mini-lathes specifically:

*The Mini-Lathe* (Workshop Practice Series 43), David Fenner

*Mini-lathe Tools and Projects* (Workshop Practice Series 48), David Fenner

General works on lathes and turning that are worth reading include:

*Metal Turning on the Lathe* (Crowood Metalworking Guides), David Clark

*The Amateur's Lathe* (Special Interest Model Books), Lawrence H. Sparey

*Using the Small Lathe* (Model and Allied Publications), Leonard C. Mason

The Crowood *Metalworking Series* contains several other titles that will be useful to anyone with an interest in hobby engineering.

## Periodicals

*Model Engineers' Workshop* is a monthly magazine has its focus on tools and techniques in the home workshop. It has carried articles on numerous aspects of running a mini-lathe, including designs for many accessories.

*Model Engineer* is a bi-weekly publication that has more emphasis on model making than its sister publication, but still has published many useful articles on mini-lathes.

*Metalworker's Workshop* and *Home Shop Machinist* are two American magazines that cover similar ground to MEW and ME. Although they have much in common, the content has a distinctly different 'transatlantic flavour'.

## Websites

www.model-engineer.co.uk is the busiest UK forum for model and hobby engineering, covering all aspects of the hobby. Very friendly and welcoming for new members and probably one of the best places to seek advice.

http://mikesworkshop.weebly.com is a website set up by Mike Cox and is one of the few British websites dedicated largely to mini-lathes, their use and modification.

www.mini-lathe.org.uk is another British site dedicated to mini-lathes. Although it does not have a huge amount of content, there is some useful advice there.

www.mini-lathe.com is an American website set up in 2000 by Frank Hoose. It contains a wealth of information on mini-lathes, including a visit to the SIEG factory in China.

The original mini-lathe users' group on Yahoo was set up in 1999 but it seems to have 'lost its way'. You may like to take a look at two more recent groups dedicated to mini-lathes, if you don't mind signing up to Yahoo. The first is a general group, the second is dedicated to mini-lathe modifications:

https://groups.yahoo.com/neo/groups/7x12minilathe/info

https://groups.yahoo.com/neo/groups/mlathemods/info

www.homews.co.uk is the personal website of former *Model Engineers' Workshop* editor Harold Hall. It has a great deal of valuable information for hobby engineers, although it is not specific to mini-lathes.

# *Index*